Vegetarian Slow Cooker Recipes: Top 71 Quick & Easy Vegetarian Crockpot Recipe Book

By Maria Holmes

All Rights Reserved. No part of this publication may be reproduced in any form or by any means, including scanning, photocopying, or otherwise without prior written permission of the copyright holder. Copyright © 2013

Cover photo: © Serghei Velusceac - Fotolia.com & © Kitch Bain - Fotolia.com

All information in this book has been carefully researched and checked for factual accuracy. However, the author and publishers make no warranty, express or implied, that the information contained herein is appropriate for every individual, situation or purpose, and assume no responsibility for errors or omissions. The reader assumes the risk and full responsibility for all actions, and the authors will not be held responsible for any loss or damage, whether consequential, incidental, special or otherwise that may result from the information presented in this publication.

The author has relied on her own experience as well as many different sources for this book, and has done her best to check the facts and to give credit where it is due. In the event that any material is incorrect or has been used without proper permission, please contact the author so that the oversight can be corrected at:
HolmesCookedMeals@gmail.com

Table of Contents

Preface 1
Acknowledgement 3
Slow Cooker Tips 4
Top 10 Slow Cooker Tips 7
Appetizers 9
Drinks 19
Breakfast 30
Soups 37
Chili and Stews 47
Sides 56
Entrées 67
Desserts 87
Fondues 112
Potluck 122
Conclusion 139

Preface

Dear Reader!

I would like to take this opportunity to thank you for taking the time to read my book and hope that you find these vegetarian slow cooker recipes interesting and tasty!

Before we start exploring how you can prepare these great slow cooker vegetarian meals, I would like to introduce myself. My name is Maria Holmes and I am indeed the author of the slow cooker recipe book that you are now reading. If you are interested in learning more about me, my mission and my passion, please join my Facebook community at **Homes Cooked Meals** for interesting activities and enthusiastic discussions. Or you might want to visit my blog at www.holmescookedmeals.com.

But let's get back to the topic at hand - *Vegetarian Slow Cooker Recipes: Top 71 Quick & Easy Vegetarian Crockpot Recipe Book*.

In this cookbook, you will discover the amazing versatility of the slow cooker! If you thought that the slow cooker was designed only for meat-eaters, the *Vegetarian Slow Cooker Recipes: Top 71 Quick & Easy Vegetarian Crockpot Recipe Book* will introduce you to amazing vegetarian slow cooked meals. And if you're already a slow cooker enthusiast, you will find an entirely new selection of healthy, delicious recipes that you can easily make in your favorite appliance.

Slow cookers are useful for much more than transforming an inexpensive cut of meat into a delicious meal. They are great for cooking healthy vegetarian meals since they provide a foolproof way to cook perfect beans, grains, vegetables, and so much more. Most slow cooker cookbooks are meat oriented and rely heavily on processed or preserved ingredients. This cookbook tries to change all that by placing more reliance on fresh ingredients and amazing combinations of spices.

This cookbook was written for everyone who needs to make easy meals without sacrificing full flavor or health.

So get ready to discover all the tasty simmered-in flavors of slow cooking.

Enjoy and be well!

Maria Holmes

Acknowledgement

I would like to express my gratitude to my parents, who have always supported and encouraged me in everything I have done in my life. Without their love and support, this book might never have been written.

I am also grateful to my dear friends who I often use as test subjects when developing my recipes. Without their help and sacrifice, many of these recipes may have turned out bland and tasteless. Many of these friends have become members and supporters of my Holmes Cooked Meals Facebook Page or website at www.holmescookedmeals.com.

And a special thank you goes out to my loving husband and my two amazing children (Ellie and Isaac) who endlessly encourage me to share my love for food and my many recipes with the world.

And most importantly, thank you, dear reader, for purchasing *Vegetarian Slow Cooker Recipes: Top 71 Quick & Easy Vegetarian Crockpot Recipe Book*.

Slow Cooker Tips

Whether you are new to slow cooking or have been using a slow cooker for many years, you will find these quick slow cooker tips handy.

Purchasing Your New Slow Cooker

Size:

Slow cookers come in a wide variety of sizes. When shopping for your slow cooker, keep mindful of how you will be using your cooker. For example, if you are making meals for a small family of four, a 3 quart slow cooker will suffice. But if you are preparing a pot luck meal for a crowd, you will definitely want a 6 quart slow cooker.

Shape:

A larger slow cooker should be oval shaped to facilitate fitting larger ingredients. However, for soups, stews and chili, a round slow cooker works well.

Snug-Fitting Lid:

Removing the lid during the cooking process will cause the release of a great deal of heat. Choosing a tight-fitting, clear lid will help you resist the urge to lift the lid to peek inside before the food is ready.

Removable Inserts:

It is always easier to clean a slow cooker with a removable insert than a one-piece unit. Be sure to wait until the insert has cooled before washing or you may run the risk of cracking the ceramic piece. These removable inserts are sometimes dishwasher safe, which makes cleaning even more convenient and easy.

Extra Features:

Many of the newer slow cooker models now come with programmable timers. This is a very convenient feature if you plan on being gone all day. The timer will switch the slow cooker automatically to the warm setting after the cooking is complete.

Using an Older or Hand-Me-Down Slow Cooker

Here are a few tips to remember when using an older or hand-me down slow cooker:

1) Check the capacity by filling a measuring cup with 8 ounces (1 cup) of water. Keep track of how many cups of water it takes to fill to the rim of the cooker. Remember that 2 cups equals 1 pint and 4 cups equals 1 quart.

2) Look for hot spots if you notice that your food if cooking unevenly by rotating the insert halfway through the cooking process.

3) Older models tend to cook at slightly cooler temperatures. Therefore you should test the temperature and make sure that your cooker is heating to safe temperatures by performing this test:

- Fill the slow cooker between half and two-thirds full of water.

- Cover and cook on low for 8 hours.

- Remove the lid and immediately check the temperature of the water with a thermometer. Ideally the temperature should be 185ºF. If the temperature is higher, your cooker is cooking at a faster rate. Check the food for doneness earlier than the recipe indicates. A lower temperature indicates food-safety risks, so it's time for a new slow cooker.

4) External timer devices are available for older models. The timer plugs into the wall outlet, and the cooker plugs into the timer. When the cooking time expires, the timer automatically switches to warm.

Choosing the Right Recipe

1) Pick recipes that fit your day. Are you rushing to feed the kids' breakfast and get out the door? Then you may want to add the ingredients to the insert the night before, refrigerate, and turn on as you leave for work. But be aware that cooking time may need to increase when starting with cold ingredients.

2) It is better to let your cooker cook on LOW than to set a timer that shuts off the cooker early in the afternoon. Do not leave your food in a slow cooker that has been turned off for more than 4 hours.

3) In addition to chili, slow cookers are perfect for simmering stew or soup. They can even be used for casual dips and decadent desserts.

Cleaning Your Slow Cooker

Always unplug the slow cooker and let the insert cool completely before washing it. Extreme temperature changes may cause the ceramic insert to crack.

For easy cleanup, buy clear, heavy-duty plastic liners made to fit 3 to 6-1/2 quart oval and round slow cookers. Place the plastic liner inside the slow cooker before adding the ingredients. After the cooker has cooled, all you have to do is throw the liner away.

If not using liners, be sure to spray the inside of the slow cooker with cooking spray before placing the food inside.

When cleaning a one-piece slow cooker, never immerse the unit in water. Instead, unplug the unit and wipe it clean with a cloth.

Top 10 Slow Cooker Tips

1) Adjust the cooking times to accommodate higher altitudes. Water boils at a lower temperature, making food cook more slowly at altitudes above 3,500 feet. Try cooking meats on the high heat setting. For vegetables, cut smaller pieces than directed. Check food temperatures with a thermometer to guarantee your food is safe to eat.

2) Resist the urge to stir! Opening the lid releases a great deal of heat, increasing the cooking time. Following directions precisely and layering ingredients in the order instructed contribute to the success of the dish.

3) If you have the time, choose to cook recipes on the low setting. You are more likely to achieve tender, moist, and flavorful meals.

4) Use a heavy duty aluminum foil to make removing recipes a cinch. Simply fold the foil until you have a six-layer foil rectangle. Press the folded foil on the edge of the slow cooker insert. Next place the aluminum foil lengthwise and widthwise so that the foil covers the bottom of the insert and hangs over the edge. Use the overhanging edges to pull out the meals that should remain intact.

5) Avoid mushy vegetables. Be sure to cut veggies uniformly so that they cook evenly. If you find your vegetables are overdone, try cooking them in a foil packet for part of the cooking time.

6) Do not overcrowd a cooker. Fill the slow cooker half to two-thirds full. This will ensure that meat reaches a safe temperature quickly and food cooks evenly.

7) Overcooking is possible, especially with casseroles. Make sure to keep an eye on meals during the last hour of cooking and test with a thermometer for complete doneness.

8) Thicken the sauce in the last 20 to 30 minutes of cooking. Simply remove the lid and cook on high to finish the meal.

9) It's easy to double or halve recipes for a slow cooker, just be sure to use a cooker of suitable size for the change in recipe.

10) To avoid mushy noodles, cook pasta separately in boiling water according to package direction. Add the pasta to the slow cooker 30 minutes before the meal is done unless otherwise indicated.

Appetizers

RECIPES

Spicy Vegetable Chili con Queso 10
Mozzarella Marinara Spread 12
Creamy White Bean Spread 13
Hoisin-Garlic Mushrooms with Red Sweet Peppers 15
Lemony Artichoke Dip with Creamy Swiss Cheese 17

Spicy Vegetable Chili con Queso

With 3 kinds of beans, 2 kinds of squash, and a lot of cheese, this dip will provide you with a tempting change of pace.

Preparation time: 20 minutes
Cooking time: 6 to 7 hours (LOW) or 3 to 3-1/2 hours (HIGH)

Ingredients

1 can (15-ounce) pinto beans, rinsed and drained
1 can (15-ounce) black beans, rinsed and drained
1 can (15-ounce) chili beans with chili gravy, undrained
1 can (10-ounce) chopped tomatoes and green chile peppers, undrained
1 medium zucchini, chopped (about 1-1/4 cups)
1-1/4 cups chopped yellow summer squash
1 large sweet onion, chopped (about 1 cup)
1/4 cup tomato paste
1 fresh jalapeno pepper, seeded and finely chopped
2 to 3 teaspoons chili powder
4 cloves garlic, minced
3 cups Mexican blend shredded cheese (about 12-ounces)
Tortilla or corn chips

Directions

In a 3-1/2 or 4 quart slow cooker, combine all ingredients except the Mexican blend shredded cheese.

Cover and cook on LOW for 6 to 7 hours or on HIGH for 3 to 3-1/2 hours. Stir in the Mexican blend shredded cheese until melted.

Serve immediately or keep warm, covered on WARM or LOW setting for up to 1 hour.

Serve with tortilla chips.

Makes about 32 appetizer servings.

Per 1/4 cup (without dippers)

Calories: 81; Fat: 4g; Cholesterol: 9mg; Sodium: 231mg; Carbohydrate: 8g; Fiber: 2g; Protein: 5g

Mozzarella Marinara Spread

As an alternative to dipping mozzarella sticks into a marinara dipping sauce, why not combine the cheese with the sauce and create a hot and hearty appetizer?

Preparation time: 5 minutes
Cooking time: 2 hours (LOW) plus 30 minutes on LOW

Ingredients

2 cups chunky marinara sauce
8 ounces fresh mozzarella cheese, cut into cubes
2 tablespoons chopped fresh basil leaves
2 loaves (10-ounce, each) baguette French bread, cut into 1/4-inch slices, toasted

Directions

Spray a 1 to 2 quart slow cooker with cooking spray.

Pour the marinara sauce into the slow cooker.

Cover and cook on LOW for 2 hours or until hot.

Stir the mozzarella cheese and basil into the marinara sauce.

Cover and cook for an additional 30 minutes or until the cheese is just starting to melt.

Serve the spread with the French bread slices.

Makes 24 servings.

Per Serving (2 tablespoons spread and 4 bread slices)

Calories: 110; Fat: 3g; Cholesterol: 0mg; Sodium: 290mg; Carbohydrate: 16g; Fiber: 1g; Protein: 5g

Creamy White Bean Spread

Whether served warm or at room temperature, this spread tastes terrific. If you'd like to make it ahead, chill it and then return it to room temperature before serving.

Preparation time: 15 minutes
Cooking time: 3 to 4 hours (LOW)

Ingredients

2 cans (15-ounce, each) Great Northern or cannelloni (white kidney) beans, rinsed and drained
1/2 cup vegetable broth
1 tablespoons olive oil
3 cloves garlic, minced
1 teaspoon snipped fresh marjoram or 1/4 teaspoon dried marjoram, crushed
1/2 teaspoon snipped fresh rosemary or 1/8 teaspoon dried rosemary, crushed
1/8 teaspoon ground black pepper
Olive oil
Fresh marjoram leaves and rosemary (optional)
Pita Chips or assorted crackers

Directions

In a 1-1/2 quart slow cooker, combine the beans, vegetable broth, 1 tablespoon olive oil, garlic, marjoram, rosemary, and ground black pepper.

Cover and cook on LOW for 3 to 4 hours (do not use the high-heat setting).

To serve, slightly mash the bean mixture using a potato masher and spoon the bean mixture into a serving bowl. If desired, drizzle with additional olive oil and/or sprinkle with fresh marjoram leaves and rosemary.

Serve warm or at room temperature with Pita Chips or assorted crackers.

Makes about 20 appetizer servings.

Pita Chips: Preheat the oven to 350ºF. Split two pita bread rounds horizontally in half and cut each circle into 6 wedges. Place the pita wedges in a single layer on a large baking sheet. In a small bowl, combine 2 tablespoons olive oil, 2 teaspoons snipped fresh oregano, and 1/4 teaspoon kosher salt.

Brush the pita wedges with the oil mixture. Bake for 12 to 15 minutes or until crisp and light brown.

Remove from the baking sheet and cool on a wire rack.

Makes 24 chips.

Per 2 tablespoons (without pita chips)

Calories: 70; Fat: 1g; Cholesterol: 0mg; Sodium: 33mg; Carbohydrate: 11g; Fiber: 3g; Protein: 4g

Hoisin-Garlic Mushrooms with Red Sweet Peppers

No need to visit a specialty store for hoisin. Look for the salty, sweet, and slightly spicy sauce in the Asian section of most supermarkets.

Preparation time: 15 minutes
Cooking time: 5 to 6 hours (LOW) or 2-1/2 to 3 hours (HIGH)

Ingredients

1/2 cup bottled hoisin sauce
1/4 cup water
2 tablespoons minced garlic (6 cloves)
1/4 to 1/2 teaspoon crushed red pepper
24 ounces whole fresh button mushrooms, trimmed
1 large red sweet pepper, seeded and cut into chunks

Directions

In a 3-1/2 or 4 quart slow cooker, combine the hoisin sauce, water, garlic, and crushed red pepper.

Add the mushrooms and sweet pepper chunks, stirring to coat with the sauce.

Cover and cook on LOW for 5 to 6 hours or on HIGH got 2-1/2 to 3 hours.

Using a slotted spoon, remove the mushrooms and pepper chunks from the slow cooker and discard the sauce.

Serve with decorative toothpicks

Makes 10 servings.

Per Serving

Calories: 51; Fat: 1g; Cholesterol: 0mg; Sodium: 211mg; Carbohydrate: 9g; Fiber: 10g; Protein: 3g

Lemony Artichoke Dip with Creamy Swiss Cheese

Creamy Swiss cheese and sweet red peppers envelop velvety-soft artichokes in this dip enhanced with citrus flavor.

Preparation time: 25 minutes
Cooking time: 2 to 2-1/2 hours (LOW)

Ingredients

1 tablespoon olive oil
1 cup chopped fresh mushrooms
1/4 cup chopped red sweet pepper
3 tablespoons finely chopped shallot
1 clove garlic, minced
1 carton (8-ounces) sour cream
1/2 cup cream cheese
1 teaspoon finely shredded lemon peel
1 tablespoon lemon juice
1 tablespoon Dijon-style mustard
3 jars (6-ounces, each) marinated artichoke hearts, drained and coarsely chopped
1 cup shredded Gruyère or Swiss cheese (about 4-ounce)
Toasted baguette-style French bread slices or pita chips

Directions

Heat the olive oil in a medium skillet over medium heat. Add the mushrooms, red sweet pepper, shallot, and garlic and cook the mixture, stirring frequently, until the pepper and shallot are tender.

Combine the sour cream, cream cheese, lemon peel, lemon juice, and Dijon-style mustard in a medium bowl. Stir in the mushroom mixture, artichoke hearts, and Gruyère cheese.

Spoon the artichoke mixture into a 1-1/2 to 2 quart slow cooker.

Cover and cook on LOW for 2 to 2-1/2 hours or until heated through.

Serve immediately or keep warm, covered, on WARM or LOW setting for up to 2 hours.

Stir before serving and serve with toasted French bread slices or pita chips.

Makes 32 (2 tablespoon) servings.

Per Serving

Calories: 71; Fat: 6g; Cholesterol: 9mg; Sodium: 105mg; Carbohydrate: 2g; Fiber: 0g; Protein: 2g

Drinks

RECIPES

Hot Wine to Warm You 20
Warmed Spiced Citrus Cider 22
Spicy Aztec Chili Hot Chocolate 24
Warm Mulled Cranberry Punch 26
Hot Zombies..28

Hot Wine to Warm You

Cut the fresh ginger into nickel-size slices. Store any remaining unpeeled fresh ginger in a resealable plastic bag in the freezer.

Preparation time: 15 minutes
Cooking time: 4 to 5 hours (LOW) or 2 to 2-1/2 hours (HIGH)

Ingredients

1 orange
1 lemon
4 slices fresh ginger
3 inch cinnamon stick, broken
8 whole allspice
8 whole cloves
1 750-milliliter bottle Bordeaux or Beaujolais wine
4 cups water
1 can (12-ounce) frozen pineapple-orange juice concentrate
1/2 cup brandy
1/2 cup sugar
1/4 cup Triple Sec or other orange liqueur
Orange slices and/or cinnamon sticks

Directions

Use a vegetable peeler to cut several wide strips of peel from the orange and lemon, avoiding the white pith underneath. Cut the orange and lemon in half and juice the orange and lemon over a small bowl.

For the spice bag, cut a 6 inch square from a double thickness of 100% cotton cheesecloth. Place the lemon peel strips, orange peel strips, ginger, the broken cinnamon stick, allspice, and cloves in the center of the cloth. Bring the corners together and tie closed with 100% cotton kitchen string.

In a 4 or 5 quart slow cooker, combine the spice bag, wine, water, pineapple-orange juice concentrate, brandy, sugar, Triple Sec, and citrus juices.

Cover and cook on LOW setting for 4 to 5 hours or on HIGH for 2 to 2-1/2 hours.

Discard the spice bag.

Serve immediately or keep warm, covered on WARM or LOW setting for up to 2 hours.

To serve, ladle the beverage into heatproof mugs or cups and garnish with orange slices and/or cinnamon sticks.

Makes about 22 (4 ounce) servings.

Per Serving

Calories: 103; Fat: 0g; Cholesterol: 0mg; Sodium: 8mg; Carbohydrate: 15g; Fiber: 0g; Protein: 0g

Warmed Spiced Citrus Cider

Adults love this mildly spiced non-alcoholic party potion nearly as much as kids do.

Preparation time: 10 minutes
Cooking time: 5 to 6 hours (LOW) or 2-1/2 to 3 hours (HIGH)

Ingredients

8 cups apple cider or juice
1 cup orange juice *
1/2 cup lemon juice *
1/4 cup honey
8 inch cinnamon stick, broken
8 whole cloves
3 slices fresh ginger

Directions

In a 3-1/2 or 4 quart slow cooker, combine the apple cider, orange juice, lemon juice, and honey. Stir to dissolve the honey.

For the spice bag, cut a 6 inch square from a double thickness or 100% cotton cheesecloth. Place the broken cinnamon stick, cloves, and ginger in the center of the cloth. Bring the corners together and tie closed with 100% cotton kitchen string. Add the spice bag to the juice mixture in the slow cooker.

Cover and cook on LOW for 5 to 6 hours or on HIGH for 2-1/2 to 3 hours.

Discard the spice bag.

Serve immediately or keep warm, covered, on WARM or LOW setting for up to 2 hours.

To serve, ladle the beverage into heatproof mugs or cups.

Makes about 13 (6-ounce) servings.

* Tip: If you squeeze fresh oranges and lemons for the juice, use a vegetable peeler to cut several wide strips of peel from the fruit, avoiding the white pith underneath. Add the peel to the spice bag.

Per Serving

Calories: 89; Fat: 9g; Cholesterol: 0mg; Sodium: 1mg; Carbohydrate: 10g; Fiber: 0g; Protein: 0g

Spicy Aztec Chili Hot Chocolate

Cinnamon and chile pepper add zip to a drink so rich and creamy, it's almost like dessert.

Preparation time: 15 minutes
Cooking time: 4 hours (LOW) or 2 hours (HIGH)

Ingredients

4 cups milk
2 cups half-and-half or whole milk
1-1/2 cups semisweet chocolate pieces
1 teaspoon instant espresso coffee powder
1 teaspoon ground cinnamon
1/2 teaspoon ground chipotle chile pepper
Ground cinnamon (optional)
Chocolate curls (optional)

Directions

In a 3-1/2 or 4 quart slow cooker, combine the milk, half-and-half, chocolate pieces, espresso coffee powder, ground cinnamon, and ground chipotle chile pepper.

Cover and cook on LOW for 4 hours or on HIGH for 2 hours, whisking vigorously once halfway through the cooking time.

Serve immediately or keep warm, covered, on WARM or LOW setting for up to 2 hours.

Before serving, whisk well and ladle the hot chocolate into heatproof mugs or cups. If desired, sprinkle each serving with cinnamon and/or chocolate curls.

Makes 12 (4-ounce) servings.

Per Servings

Calories: 197; Fat: 13g; Cholesterol: 21mg; Sodium: 53mg; Carbohydrate: 19g; Fiber: 1g; Protein: 5g

Warm Mulled Cranberry Punch

Make this spicy but sweet drink more diet-friendly by using low-calorie cranberry juice.

Preparation time: 15 minutes
Cooking time: 4 to 6 hours (LOW) or 2 to 2-1/2 hours (HIGH)

Ingredients

1 orange
8 inch cinnamon stick, broken
8 whole cloves
4 whole allspice
1 bottle (32-ounces) cranberry juice
1 can (11-1/2-ounce) frozen white grape-raspberry juice concentrate
4 cups water

Directions

Use a vegetable peeler to cut several wide strips of peel from the orange, avoiding the white pith underneath. Cut the orange in half and juice it over a small bowl.

For the spice bag, cut a 6-inch square form a double thickness of 100% cotton cheesecloth. Place the orange peel, broken cinnamon stick, cloves, and allspice in the center of the cloth. Bring the corners together and tie closed with 100% cotton kitchen string.

In a 3-1/2 or 4 quart slow cooker, combine the spice bag, cranberry juice, grape-raspberry juice concentrate, water, and the orange juice.

Cover and cook on LOW for 4 to 6 hours or on HIGH for 2 to 2-1/2 hours.

Discard the spice bag.

Serve immediately or keep warm, covered, on WARM or LOW setting for up to 2 hours.

To serve, ladle the beverage into heatproof mugs or cups.

Makes about 12 (6-ounce) servings.

Per Serving

Calories: 114; Fat: 0g; Cholesterol: 0mg; Sodium: 7mg; Carbohydrate: 29g; Fiber: 1g; Protein: 0g

Hot Zombies

Better to drink one than to meet one, right? Think of a Hot Zombie as a tropical hot toddy, sprinkled with rum and brandy and laced with pineapple, Maraschino cherries, and lemon.

Preparation time: 15 minutes
Cooking time: 4 to 5 hours (LOW) or 2 to 2-1/2 hours (HIGH)

Ingredients

1 can (15-1/4-ounce) pineapple slices (juice pack)
1 jar (6-ounces) Maraschino cherries
1 carton (59-ounces) pineapple-orange-banana juice
1-1/4 cups dark rum
1/2 cup apricot brandy or cherry brandy
1 lemon, halved, seeded and thinly sliced

Directions

Drain the pineapple slices, reserving the juice. Cut the pineapple slices in half crosswise.

Drain the cherries, reserving the juice and refrigerate the cherry juice until needed.

In a 5 to 6 quart slow cooker, combine the pineapple slices, reserved pineapple juice, drained Maraschino cherries, pineapple-orange-banana juice, dark rum, and apricot brandy.

Cover and cook on LOW for 4 to 5 hours or on HIGH for 2 to 2-1/2 hours (do not boil).

Ladle the mixture into mugs and drizzle each serving with some of the reserved cherry juice and garnish with a lemon slice.

Makes 12 (about 8-ounce) servings.

Per Serving

Calories: 194; Fat: 0g; Cholesterol: 0mg; Sodium: 7mg; Carbohydrate: 30g; Fiber: 1g; Protein: 1g

Breakfast

RECIPES

Sherried Fruit Compote 31
Cranberry and Maple Syrup Oatmeal with Pears 33
Fruit and Whole-Grain Breakfast Cereal..34
Breakfast Prunes with Orange Marmalade..35
Hazelnut-Pear Oatmeal 36

Sherried Fruit Compote

Use this compote-like dish as an alternative to syrup on French toast, waffles, and pancakes. Refrigerate the leftovers to serve with pound cake or ice cream.

Preparation time: 25 minutes
Cooking time: 3-1/2 to 4 hours (LOW) or 1-1/2 to 2 hours (HIGH)

Ingredients

1 can (20-ounce) pineapple chunks (juice pack), undrained
3 medium firm ripe plums, pitted and cut into thick wedges
2 medium cooking apples, cored and cut into 1-inch pieces
2 medium pears, cored and cut into 1-inch pieces
1/2 cup dried apricots, halved
1/3 cup packed brown sugar
1/4 cup butter, melted
1/4 cup sherry
2 tablespoons quick-cooking tapioca, crushed
1/4 teaspoon salt

Directions

Combine the pineapple, plums, apples, pears, and apricots in a 3-1/2 or 4 quart slow cooker.

Combine the brown sugar, butter, sherry, tapioca, and salt in a small bowl.

Pour the brown sugar mixture over the fruits in the slow cooker and stir to combine.

Cover and cook on LOW for 3-1/2 to 4 hours or on HIGH for 1-1/2 to 2 hours.

Makes 12 to 14 servings.

Per Serving

Calories: 148; Fat: 4g; Cholesterol: 10mg; Sodium: 79mg; Carbohydrate: 28g; Fiber: 2g; Protein: 1g

Cranberry and Maple Syrup Oatmeal with Pears

Friends who try to eat healthy will thank you twice. First for offering something filled with whole grain goodness and then for making it taste so good.

Preparation time: 15 minutes
Cooking time: 6 to 7 hours (LOW)

Ingredients

Nonstick cooking spray
4-3/4 cups water
1-1/2 cups steel-cut oats
3/4 cup pure maple syrup
1/3 cup golden raisins
1/3 cup dried cranberries
1/3 cup chopped dried pears
1 teaspoon ground cinnamon or five-spice powder
1 teaspoon vanilla
1/2 teaspoon salt

Directions

Lightly coat the inside of a 3-1/2 or 4 quart slow cooker with the cooking spray.

Combine all the ingredients in the prepared slow cooker.

Cover and cook on LOW for 6 to 7 hours.

Makes 8 servings.

Per Serving

Calories: 242; Fat: 2g; Cholesterol: 0mg; Sodium: 154mg; Carbohydrate: 56g; Fiber: 4g; Protein: 5g

Fruit and Whole-Grain Breakfast Cereal

Cereals made with whole-grain have generally been linked to health benefits, like a lower risk of death from heart disease. Whole grain-rich cereals lower the risk of gaining weight or having a higher body mass index (BMI).

Preparation time: 15 minutes
Cooking time: 6 to 7 hours (LOW) or 3 to 3-1/2 hours (HIGH)

Ingredients

5 cups water
2 cups uncooked whole-grain cereal of your choice
1 medium apple, peeled and chopped
1 cup unsweetened apple juice
1/4 cup dried apricots, chopped
1/4 cup dried cranberries
1/4 cup raisins
1/4 cup chopped dates
2 to 4 tablespoons maple syrup, to desired sweetness
1 teaspoon ground cinnamon
1/2 teaspoon salt

Directions

Combine all the ingredients in a 4 to 6 quart slow cooker.

Cover and cook on LOW for 6 to 7 hours or on HIGH for 3 to 3-1/2 hours, or until the fruits and grains are as soft as you like them.

Makes 10 servings.

Per Serving

Calories: 185; Fat: 2g; Cholesterol: 0mg; Sodium: 122mg; Carbohydrate: 56g; Fiber: 40g; Protein: 5g

Breakfast Prunes with Orange Marmalade

Prunes are high in vitamin A and beta-carotene (a natural antioxidant). These two vitamins play a key role in maintaining healthy eye-sight and are also used to fight acne, resulting in a smooth radiant skin.

Preparation time: 15 minutes
Cooking time: 8 to 10 hours (LOW) or 4 to 5 hours (HIGH)

Ingredients

2 cups orange juice
1/4 cup orange marmalade
1 teaspoon ground cinnamon
1/4 teaspoon ground cloves
1/4 teaspoon ground nutmeg
1 cup water
1 package (12-ounces) pitted dried prunes (approximately 1-3/4 cups)
2 thin lemon slices

Directions

Combine the orange juice, orange marmalade, cinnamon, cloves, nutmeg, and water in a 2 quart slow cooker.

Stir in the prunes and lemon slices.

Cover and cook on LOW for 8 to 10 hours or on HIGH for 4 to 5 hours.

Serve warm as a breakfast meal or chilled as a side dish with a meal later in the day.

Makes 6 servings.

Per Serving

Calories: 123; Fat: 0g; Cholesterol: 0mg; Sodium: 18mg; Carbohydrate: 30g; Fiber: 1g; Protein: 1g

Hazelnut-Pear Oatmeal

When you take a bite, you will find that the oatmeal is crisp and caramelized on top, yet nutty and moist in the middle. Your spoonful will finish with the sweet pears.

Preparation time: 15 minutes
Cooking time: 8 hours (LOW)

Ingredients

3 cups milk
3 cups water
2 cups uncooked dry regular oats
1/3 cup brown sugar
1/4 cup butter, cut into small pieces
1 teaspoon salt
1/4 teaspoon ground nutmeg
3 firm, ripe, Bartlett-pears, peeled, cored, and cut into 1/2-inch cubes (about 2-1/4 cups)
1/2 cup honey
1/2 cup chopped hazelnut, toasted

Directions

Combine all the ingredients, except for the honey and hazelnuts in a 3-1/2 or 4 quart slow cooker.

Cover and cook on LOW for 8 hours or until the oats are tender.

Spoon the oatmeal into bowls and drizzle each serving with honey and sprinkle with toasted hazelnuts.

Makes 5 servings.

Per Serving

Calories: 526; Fat: 19g; Cholesterol: 36mg; Sodium: 601mg;
Carbohydrate: 83g; Fiber: 8g; Protein: 11g

Soups

RECIPES

Vegetable Tortellini 38
Vegetable Minestrone 40
Creamy Leek and Potato 42
Squash and Apple Bisque 44
Potato and Double Corn Chowder 46

Vegetable Tortellini

Try substituting spinach tortellini. You can also use ravioletti (small ravioli that just fit in your spoon).

Preparation time: 10 minutes
Cooking time: 7 hours (LOW) or 3-1/2 hours (HIGH), plus 18 minutes on HIGH

Ingredients

2 packages (8-ounces, each) refrigerated pre-chopped celery, onion, and bell pepper mix
1/2 teaspoon pepper
1 medium zucchini, coarsely chopped
1 container (32-ounces) vegetable broth
1 package (16-ounces) frozen baby corn, bean, pea, and carrot mix
1 can (15-1/2-ounce) cannellini beans, drained
1 can (14-1/2-ounce) diced tomatoes with basil, oregano, and garlic, undrained
1 package (9-ounces) refrigerated cheese tortellini
Shredded Parmesan cheese *

* Since Parmesan cheese is made with rennet, which is derived from the stomach of slaughtered cows, some vegetarians may choose not to utilize it. You may instead substitute the Parmesan cheese for nutritional yeast.

Directions

Coat a large non-stick skillet with cooking spray and heat over medium-high heat. Add the celery, onion and bell pepper mixture, and sauté for 5 minutes or until tender.

Transfer the mixture to a 5 quart slow cooker and stir in the pepper, zucchini, vegetable broth, baby corn mixture, cannellini beans, and tomatoes with basil.

Cover and cook on LOW for 7 hours or on HIGH for 3-1/2 hours.

Increase the heat to HIGH and add the tortellini. Cover and cook for an additional 18 minutes or until the pasta is tender.

Garnish with shredded Parmesan cheese (or nutritional yeast), if desired.

Makes 6 servings.

Per Serving

Calories: 256; Fat: 1g; Cholesterol: 12mg; Sodium: 1,268mg; Carbohydrate: 48g; Fiber: 10g; Protein: 11g

Vegetable Minestrone

Minestrone is often lauded for its hearty qualities (the name means "big soup"), and all you need to transform this "big soup" into a "big meal" is a few thick slices of a seedy whole-grain bread.

Preparation time: 20 minutes
Cooking time: 7 to 9 hours (LOW) or 3-1/2 to 4-1/2 hours (HIGH), plus 15 to 20 minutes on HIGH

Ingredients

1 medium yellow summer squash, cut lengthwise in half, then cut crosswise into 1-inch pieces
2 medium carrots, cut into 1/4-inch slices (about 1 cup)
1 medium bell pepper, chopped (about 1 cup)
1 cup snap pea pods
1/3 cup chopped onion
4 cups water
1 jar (25-1/2-ounces) marinara sauce
1 can (15 to 16-ounce) kidney beans, rinsed and drained
1-1/2 cups uncooked rotini pasta (about 4-1/2-ounces)
1 teaspoon sugar
1 teaspoon salt
1/4 teaspoon pepper
Shredded Parmesan cheese, if desired *

* Since Parmesan cheese is made with rennet, which is derived from the stomach of slaughtered cows, some vegetarians may choose not to utilize it. You may instead substitute the Parmesan cheese for nutritional yeast.

Directions

Mix the squash, carrots, bell pepper, pea pods, onion, water, marinara sauce, and kidney beans in a 3-1/2 to 6 quart slow cooker.

Cover and cook on LOW for 7 to 9 hours or on HIGH for 3-1/2 to 4-1/2 hours, or until the vegetables are tender.

Stir in the rotini pasta, sugar, salt and pepper.

Cover and cook on HIGH for an additional 15 to 20 minutes, or until the pasta is tender.

Sprinkle each serving with Parmesan cheese (or nutritional yeast), if desired.

Makes 8 servings.

Per Serving

Calories: 260; Fat: 4g; Cholesterol: 0mg; Sodium: 920mg; Carbohydrate: 53g; Fiber: 7g; Protein: 10g

Creamy Leek and Potato

This is really an all-season soup. Serve it warm on a chilly evening, or chill it in the summer to get a delicious, refreshing chilled soup that is ready to be enjoyed on the deck.

Preparation time: 20 minutes
Cooking time: 8 to 10 hours (LOW) or 4 to 5 hours (HIGH), plus 20 to 30 minutes on LOW

Ingredients

6 medium leeks (about 2 pounds), thinly sliced
4 medium potatoes (about 1-1/2 pounds), cut into 1/2-inch cubes
2 cans (14-1/2-ounce, each) vegetable broth
1/4 cup margarine or butter
1/2 teaspoon salt
1/4 teaspoon pepper
1 cup half-and-half
Chopped fresh chives, if desired

Directions

Mix all the ingredients except for the half-and-half and chives in a 3-1/2 to 6 quart slow cooker.

Cover and cook on LOW for 8 to 10 hours or HIGH for 4 to 5 hours or until the vegetables are tender.

Pour the vegetable mixture by batches into a blender or food processor. Cover and blend on high speed until smooth and then return to the slow cooker. Stir in the half-and-half.

Cover and cook on LOW for an additional 20 to 30 minutes or until hot.

Sprinkle with chives.

Makes 8 servings.

Per Serving

Calories: 190; Fat: 10g; Cholesterol: 10mg; Sodium: 720mg; Carbohydrate: 22g; Fiber: 3g; Protein: 6g

Squash and Apple Bisque

Serve this bisque thoroughly chilled and enjoy a delightfully tasty treat. For extra flavor, garnish the bisque with thin slices of Granny Smith apples and sprinkle some finely chopped crystallized ginger.

Preparation time: 15 minutes
Cooking time: 8 to 10 hours (LOW) or 3 to 5 hours (HIGH), plus 15 minutes on LOW

Ingredients

1 butternut squash (about 2 pounds), peeled and cubed
1 medium onion, chopped (about 1/2 cup)
1 can (14-1/2-ounce) vegetable broth
2 cups applesauce
1/2 teaspoon ground ginger
1/4 teaspoon salt
1 cup sour cream

Directions

Mix all the ingredients except the sour cream in a 3-1/2 to 6 quart slow cooker.

Cover and cook on LOW for 8 to 10 hours or on HIGH for 3 to 5 hours, or until the squash is tender.

Place one-third to one-half of the mixture at a time in a blender or food processor. Cover and blend on high speed until smooth and then return the mixture to the slow cooker.

Stir in the sour cream, cover and cook on LOW for an additional 15 minutes or just until the soup is hot.

Stir and garnish each serving with a dollop of sour cream.

Makes 8 servings.

Per Serving

Calories: 140; Fat: 6g; Cholesterol: 20mg; Sodium: 330mg; Carbohydrate: 19g; Fiber: 2g; Protein: 3g

Potato and Double Corn Chowder

This heavenly and hearty chowder is so easy to make and tastes absolutely delicious.

Preparation time: 15 minutes
Cooking time: 6 to 8 hours (LOW) or 3 to 4 hours (HIGH)

Ingredients

1 bag (16-ounces) frozen hash brown potatoes, thawed (about 4 cups)
1 can (15-1/4-ounce) whole kernel corn, undrained
1 can (14-3/4-ounce) cream-style corn
1 can (12-ounce) evaporated milk
1 medium onion, chopped (about 1/2 cup)
1/2 teaspoon salt
1/2 teaspoon vegan Worcestershire sauce or soy sauce
1/4 teaspoon pepper

Directions

Mix all the ingredients into a 3-1/2 to 6 quart slow cooker.

Cover and cook on LOW for 6 to 8 hours or HIGH for 3 to 4 hours.

Makes 6 servings.

Per Serving

Calories: 305; Fat: 7g; Cholesterol: 12mg; Sodium: 1,040mg;
Carbohydrate: 55g; Fiber: 5g; Protein: 11g

Chili and Stews

RECIPES

Vegetarian Irish Stew 48
Vegetarian Gumbo 50
Easy Vegetable Chili Medley 51
Vegetarian Chili with Baked Tortilla Strips 52
Spicy Vegetable Chili 54

Vegetarian Irish Stew

Ground burger crumbles are made from soy protein and can transform any dish into a satisfying well-rounded meal. They are as versatile as they are nutritious.

Preparation time: 20 minutes
Cooking time: 8 hours (LOW) or 4 hours (HIGH)

Ingredients

1 teaspoon olive oil
1 medium onion, diced
2 tablespoon garlic, minced
6 baby or miniature red potatoes, quartered
1-1/2 cups baby carrots, cut lengthwise
1 cup cannellini beans, drained and rinsed
1/2 cup frozen peas
1-1/2 cups ground burger crumbles
3-1/2 cups vegetable broth
1/2 cup dry white wine
2 tablespoons soy sauce
1 tablespoon rice vinegar
1 teaspoon dried thyme
1 teaspoon dried rosemary
2 tablespoons cilantro, chopped
Salt and pepper to taste

Direction

Heat the olive oil in a large pan over medium heat. Add the onion and garlic and sauté until softened (about 5 minutes).

Transfer the onions and garlic into a 4 to 6 quart slow cooker and add the remaining ingredients.

Cover and cook on LOW for 8 hours or on HIGH for 4 hours.

Makes 6 servings.

Per Serving

Calories: 211; Fat: 3g; Cholesterol: 0mg; Sodium: 1,237mg; Carbohydrate: 41g; Fiber: 7g; Protein: 10g

Vegetarian Gumbo

Bring a little bit of the old south to your kitchen by making this easy slow cooker vegetarian gumbo.

Preparation time: 15 minutes
Cooking time: 6 to 8 hours (LOW) or 3 to 4 hours (HIGH)

Ingredients

2 cans (15-ounce, each) black beans, rinsed and drained
1 can (28-ounce) diced tomatoes, undrained
1 package (16-ounces) frozen loose-pack pepper stir-fry vegetables (yellow, green, and red bell peppers and onions)
2 cups frozen cut okra
2 to 3 teaspoons Cajun seasoning

Directions

Combine all the ingredients in a 3-1/2 or 4 quart slow cooker.

Cover and cook on LOW for 6 to 8 hours or on HIGH for 3 to 4 hours.

Serve with rice, if desired.

Makes 6 servings.

Per Serving

Calories: 153; Fat: 0g; Cholesterol: 0mg; Sodium: 639mg; Carbohydrate: 31g; Fiber: 10g; Protein: 12g

Easy Vegetable Chili Medley

Want an easy no hassle lunch, then make this easy vegetable chili medley ahead of time and just reheat whenever you are in the mood for a tasty and quick meal.

Preparation time: 15 minutes
Cooking time: 6 to 7 hours (LOW) or 3 to 3-1/2 hours (HIGH)

Ingredients

2 cans (15-ounce, each) diced tomatoes
2 cans (15-ounce, each) kidney beans, chickpeas, and/or black beans, rinsed and drained
1 can (15-ounce) tomato sauce
1 cup water
1 package (10-ounces) frozen whole-kernel corn
1 envelope (1-1/4-ounces) chili seasoning mix

Directions

Combine all the ingredients in a 3-1/2 or 4 quart slow cooker.

Cover and cook on LOW for 6 to 7 hours or on HIGH for 3 to 3-1/2 hours.

Makes 6 servings.

Per Serving

Calories: 218; Fat: 1g; Cholesterol: 0mg; Sodium: 1,346mg; Carbohydrate: 46g; Fiber: 10g; Protein: 13g

Vegetarian Chili with Baked Tortilla Strips

Served this bean-packed chili over a bed of hot cooked brown or white rice to make a heartier meatless meal. You decide if you want the tortilla strips on top.

Preparation time: 15 minutes
Cooking time: 5 to 6 hours (LOW) or 2-1/2 to 3 hours (HIGH)

Ingredients

Baked Tortilla Strips (see directions below)
1 can (15 or 16-ounce) spicy chili beans in sauce, undrained
1 can (15 to 16-ounce) pinto beans, undrained
1 can (15 to 16-ounce) dark red kidney beans, drained
1 can (14-1/2-ounce) chili-style chunky tomatoes, undrained
1 large onion, chopped (about 1 cup)
2 to 3 teaspoons chili powder
1/8 teaspoon ground cayenne

Directions

Prepare the Baked Tortilla Strips (see below).

Mix the remaining ingredients in a 3-1/2 to 6 quart slow-cooker.

Cover and cook on LOW for 5 to 6 hours or on HIGH for 2-1/2 to 3 hours, or until the flavors have blended.

Stir well before serving.

Spoon the chili over the tortilla strips, or sprinkle the tortilla strips on top.

Baked Tortilla Strips

Pre-heat the oven to 400°F. Cut 2 flour tortillas (8 inches in diameter) in half and cut each half crosswise into 1/2-inch strips. Place in a single layer on an ungreased cookie sheet. Bake for 10 to 12 minutes or until the strips are crisp and the edges are light brown.

Makes 6 servings.

Per Serving

Calories: 220; Fat: 2g; Cholesterol: 0mg; Sodium: 880mg; Carbohydrate: 48g; Fiber: 12g; Protein: 14g

Spicy Vegetable Chili

Two kinds of beans and oodles of vegetables yield a substantial meatless dinner – one that is delicious enough to please meat-lovers.

Preparation time: 30 minutes
Cooking time: 9 to 10 hours (LOW) or 4-1/2 to 5 hours (HIGH)

Ingredients

2 cans (28-ounce, each) diced tomatoes, undrained
2 cans (15 to 16-ounce, each) dark red kidney beans, rinsed and drained
2 cans (15 to 16-ounce, each) pinto beans, rinsed and drained
2 large onions, chopped onions (about 2 cups)
1 can (15-1/4-ounce) whole kernel corn, drained
2 medium chopped green sweet peppers (about 1-1/2 cups)
2 stalks celery, chopped (about 1 cup)
1 cup water
1 can (6-ounce) tomato paste
2 tablespoons chili powder
8 cloves garlic, minced
1 tablespoon vegan Worcestershire sauce or soy sauce
1 teaspoon ground cumin
1 teaspoon dried oregano, crushed
1 teaspoon bottled hot pepper sauce
1/4 teaspoon cayenne pepper (optional)
Sour cream (optional)

Directions

In a 6 or 7 quart slow cooker, stir together all the ingredients, except the sour cream.

Cover and cook on LOW for 9 to 10 hours or on HIGH for 4-1/2 to 5 hours.

If desired, serve the chili with some sour cream.

Makes 10 to 12 servings.

Per Serving

Calories: 244; Fat: 2g; Cholesterol: 0mg; Sodium: 916mg; Carbohydrate: 49g; Fiber: 12g; Protein: 13g

Sides

RECIPES

Spicy Chipotle-Orange Squash..57
Burgundy Mushrooms...59
Apple-Pecan Sweet Potatoes..61
Ratatouille..63
Green Bean Casserole 65

Spicy Chipotle-Orange Squash

Feel free to add extra brown sugar to offset the heat from the chipotle if it's too spicy.

Preparation time: 20 minutes
Cooking time: 3 to 4 hours (HIGH)

Ingredients

1 small buttercup or acorn squash (about 2 to 2-1/2 pounds)
1/4 cup water
3 tablespoons packed brown sugar
2 tablespoons butter or margarine, melted
1 teaspoon grated orange peel
3 tablespoons fresh orange juice
1/4 teaspoon salt
1 can (7-ounce) chipotle chile in adobo sauce, finely chopped

Directions

Spray a 5 to 6 quart slow cooker with cooking spray.

Cut the buttercup squash in half crosswise, remove the seeds and membranes.

Pour the water into the slow cooker and place the squash halves, cut side up (if necessary, cut off the pointed top so the squash stands upright).

Mix the remaining ingredients in a small bowl and pour into the squash.

Cover and cook on HIGH for 3 to 4 hours or until the squash is tender.

Cut the cooked squash in half.

Makes 9 servings.

Per Serving

Calories: 190; Fat: 7g; Cholesterol: 0mg; Sodium: 230mg; Carbohydrate: 29g; Fiber: 7g; Protein: 2g

Burgundy Mushrooms

The delicious juices left over after cooking the mushrooms can be used for a multitude of other dishes. Try thickening 1-1/2 cups liquid with 1-1/2 tablespoons all-purpose flour for a tasty sauce with French dip sandwiches. You can also pour the juices into ice cube trays, freeze, and pop out later to flavor soups or vegetables.

Preparation time: 15 minutes
Cooking time: 10 hours (LOW) or 5 hours (HIGH)

Ingredients

3 pounds fresh button mushrooms
1-1/2 cups Burgundy or other dry red wine
1 can (14-ounce) vegetable broth
1/2 cup butter, cut into pieces
1 tablespoon vegan Worcestershire sauce or soy sauce
1 teaspoon salt
1/2 teaspoon garlic powder
1/2 teaspoon dried thyme
1/2 teaspoon pepper
Fresh thyme sprigs

Directions

Place the mushrooms in a 6 quart slow cooker and add the Burgundy and all the remaining ingredients, except the fresh thyme sprigs, into the cooker.

Cover and cook on LOW for 10 hours or on HIGH for 5 hours.

Serve the mushrooms with a slotted spoon and garnish with the fresh thyme sprigs, if desired.

Makes 8 servings.

Per Serving

Calories: 156; Fat: 12g; Cholesterol: 31mg; Sodium: 662mg; Carbohydrate: 7g; Fiber: 2g; Protein: 7g

Apple-Pecan Sweet Potatoes

Many sweet potato dishes are prepared with lots of sugar and marshmallows. This creamy version is subtly sweet with a hint of tart apple – perfect for those people who prefer to truly enjoy the taste of sweet potatoes.

Preparation time: 15 minutes
Cooking time: 8 hours (LOW) or 4 hours (HIGH)

Ingredients

4 large sweet potatoes, peeled and cut into 1-1/2-inch cubes
1 large Granny Smith apple, peeled and chopped (about 1-1/2 cups)
1 cup vegetable broth
1/2 cup whipping cream
1/4 cup firmly packed light brown sugar
2 tablespoons butter
1/2 teaspoon salt
3/4 teaspoon ground cinnamon
3/4 cup chopped pecans, toasted

Directions

Combine the potatoes, apple, and vegetable broth in a 5 quart slow cooker.

Cover and cook on LOW for 8 hours or on HIGH for 4 hours, or until the potatoes are tender.

Drain and discard the vegetable broth.

Add the whipping cream, brown sugar, butter, cinnamon and beat at medium speed with an electric mixer until smooth and blended.

Stir in the pecans.

Makes 6 servings.

Per Serving

Calories: 318; Fat: 17g; Cholesterol: 21mg; Sodium: 362mg; Carbohydrate: 40g; Fiber: 6g; Protein: 4g

Ratatouille

I love ratatouille because it's so versatile and can be used to make a killer pizza, great on pasta or in a lasagna. I guess I'd better stop brainstorming and write down these recipes too!

Preparation time: 20 minutes
Cooking time: 8 hours (LOW) or 4 hours (HIGH)

Ingredients

1 large eggplant (about 1-1/2 pounds), peeled and cut into 1-inch cubes
1 large onion, chopped
2 tomatoes, chopped
1 large green bell pepper, cut into 1/2-inch pieces
1 large red bell pepper, cut into 1/2-inch pieces
3 medium zucchini, chopped
3 cloves garlic, minced
3 tablespoons olive oil
1 tablespoon capers
1 teaspoon salt
1/2 teaspoon black pepper
1/4 cup tomato paste
1 can (14-1/2-ounce) sliced black olives, drained
1/4 cup chopped fresh basil
1/2 cup shaved Parmesan cheese *

* Since Parmesan cheese is made with rennet, which is derived from the stomach of slaughtered cows, some vegetarians may choose not to utilize it. You may instead substitute the Parmesan cheese for nutritional yeast.

Directions

Combine the eggplant, onion, tomatoes, green bell pepper, red bell pepper, zucchini, garlic, olive oil, capers, salt and black pepper in a 6 quart slow cooker.

Cover and cook on LOW for 8 hours or on HIGH for 4 hours.

Stir in the tomato paste, black olives and basil.

Serve sprinkled with Parmesan cheese (or nutritional yeast).

Makes 8 to 10 servings.

Per Serving

Calories: 184; Fat: 13g; Cholesterol: 3mg; Sodium: 739mg; Carbohydrate: 15g; Fiber: 4g; Protein: 4g

Green Bean Casserole

Green bean casserole is an enduring side dish that fits in during any holiday spread. This recipe skips the can of cream of mushroom soup to make a healthier version of this classic.

Preparation time: 15 minutes
Cooking time: 4-1/2 hours (LOW)

Ingredients

2 packages (16-ounces, each) frozen French-cut green beans, thawed
1 container (10-ounces) refrigerated Alfredo sauce
1 can (8-ounce) diced water chestnuts, drained
1 jar (6-ounces) sliced mushrooms, drained
1 cup shredded Parmesan cheese (about 4 ounces) *
1/2 teaspoon freshly ground pepper
1 can (16-ounce) French fried onions, divided
1/2 cup chopped pecans

* Since Parmesan cheese is made with rennet, which is derived from the stomach of slaughtered cows, some vegetarians may choose not to utilize it. You may instead substitute the Parmesan cheese for nutritional yeast.

Directions

In a large bowl, stir together the French-cut green beans, Alfredo sauce, water chestnuts, mushrooms, Parmesan cheese (or nutritional yeast), ground pepper and 1/2 of the French fried onions.

Spoon the mixture into a lightly greased 3-1/2 or 4 quart slow cooker.

Cover and cook on LOW for 4-1/2 hours or until bubbly.

Heat the pecan and the remaining French fried onions in a small non-stick skillet over medium-low heat, stirring often for 1 to 2 minutes or until toasted and fragrant. Sprinkle the mixture over the casserole just before serving.

Makes 10 servings.

Per Serving

Calories: 461; Fat: 32g; Cholesterol: 22mg; Sodium: 543mg; Carbohydrate: 27g; Fiber: 3g; Protein: 8g

Entrées

RECIPES

South Indian Lentils with Curry Leaves 68
Pasta with Eggplant Sauce 70
Easy Vegetable Pot Pie...72
Spiced Cauliflower and Potatoes 73
Black Bean Enchilada Casserole 75
Curried Vegetables...77
Vegetarian Spaghetti Sauce 79
Winter Vegetable Risotto...81
Ultimate Macaroni and Cheese 83
Tropical Stuffed Cabbage Rolls 85

South Indian Lentils with Curry Leaves

When cooking the tarka (a mixture of cumin, mustard seeds, onion, and curry leaves) be sure the oil is hot. The mustard seeds need to pop and the curry leaves need to crackle to release their oils and give good flavor.

Preparation time: 15 minutes
Cooking time: 5-1/2 hours (LOW), plus 30 minutes (LOW)

Ingredients

3 cups dried, split, and skinned masoor dal (red lentils)
2 medium tomatoes, finely chopped (about 1 cup)
1 medium white or red onion, coarsely chopped (about 1/2 cup)
2 to 4 fresh green Thai, serrano, or cayenne chile peppers, stems removed and seeded (if desired), and finely chopped *
2 tablespoon salt
1 teaspoon ground cumin
1 teaspoon ground coriander
1/2 teaspoon ground turmeric
9 cups water
2 tablespoons vegetable or canola oil
2 teaspoons cumin seeds
1 teaspoon black or yellow mustard seeds
15 to 20 fresh curry leaves
1/4 cup finely chopped white or red onion
1 can (14-ounce) coconut milk
Hot cooked basmati rice or brown rice

Directions

Wash the dal thoroughly in a colander.

Combine the dal, tomatoes, coarsely chopped onion, chile peppers, salt, ground cumin, coriander and turmeric in a 5 quart slow cooker. Stir in the water.

Cover and cook on LOW for 5-1/2 hours.

Heat the vegetable oil in a large skillet over medium-high heat. Add the cumin seeds and mustard seeds. Cover and cook until the mustard seeds pop. Add the curry leaves and the finely chopped onion and cook, stirring until lightly brown. (Watch carefully because the curry leaves burn easily)

Stir in the mustard seeds mixture and coconut milk into the mixture in the slow cooker. Cover and cook on LOW for an additional 30 minutes.

Serve the stew over hot cooked rice.

Makes 8 servings.

* Tip: Fresh chile peppers contain volatile oils that can burn your skin and eyes. Avoid direct contact with them as much as possible. Wear disposable plastic or rubber gloves when working with fresh chiles. If you do touch the chiles with your bare hands, wash your hands and nails thoroughly with soap and warm water.

Per Serving

Calories: 531; Fat: 15g; Cholesterol: 0mg; Sodium: 1,786mg; Carbohydrate: 80g; Fiber: 12g; Protein: 22g

Pasta with Eggplant Sauce

In this vegetarian recipe, chunks of eggplant are slow-cooked in a delicious spaghetti sauce, offering you a healthy, low-calorie alternative to the typical ground beef or sausage sauces.

Preparation time: 25 minutes
Cooking time: 7 to 8 hours (LOW) or 3-1/2 to 4 hours (HIGH)

Ingredients

1 medium eggplant
2 cans (14-1/2-ounce, each) no salt-added diced tomatoes, undrained
1 can (6-ounce) Italian-style tomato paste
1 can (4-ounce) sliced mushrooms, drained
1 medium onion, chopped (about 1/2 cup)
1/4 cup dry red wine
1/4 cup water
1-1/2 teaspoons dried oregano, crushed
2 cloves garlic, minced
1/3 cup pitted Kalamata olives or ripe olives, sliced
2 tablespoons snipped fresh Italian (flat-leaf) parsley
Ground black pepper
4 cups hot cooked penne pasta
3 tablespoons grated or shredded Parmesan cheese *
2 tablespoons pine nuts, toasted (optional)

* *Since Parmesan cheese is made with rennet, which is derived from the stomach of slaughtered cows, some vegetarians may choose not to utilize it. You may instead substitute the Parmesan cheese for nutritional yeast.*

Directions

Peel the eggplant, if desired and cut into 1-inch pieces.

Combine the eggplant, tomatoes, tomato paste, mushrooms, onion, red wine, water, oregano, and garlic in a 3-1/2 to 5 quart slow cooker.

Cover and cook on LOW for 7 to 8 hours or on HIGH for 3-1/2 to 4 hours.

Stir in the olives, parsley and season to taste with ground black pepper.

Serve over hot cooked penne pasta. Sprinkle with Parmesan cheese (or nutritional yeast) and, if desired, pine nuts.

Makes 6 servings.

Per Serving

Calories: 249; Fat: 3g; Cholesterol: 2mg; Sodium: 520mg; Carbohydrate: 46g; Fiber: 6g; Protein: 9g

Easy Vegetable Pot Pie

Using frozen biscuits in this recipe makes it easy to cook the exact number of biscuits that you need.

Preparation time: 15 minutes
Cooking time: 5 hours (LOW)

Ingredients

8 small red potatoes, peeled and diced
3 carrots, chopped
2 celery ribs, chopped
1 cup sliced fresh mushrooms
1 teaspoon pepper
1/2 teaspoon celery salt
1/4 teaspoon salt
2 cans (10-3/4-ounce, each) cream of mushroom soup
1-1/4 cup frozen mixed vegetables
5 hot cooked biscuits
Chopped fresh basil

Directions

Combine all the ingredients except the biscuits and basil in a 5 quart slow cooker coated with cooking spray.

Cover and cook on LOW for 5 hours.

Spoon the vegetable mixture into bowls and top with the cooked biscuits. Garnish with fresh basil if desired.

Makes 5 servings.

Per Serving

Calories: 547; Fat: 17g; Cholesterol: 2mg; Sodium: 1,288mg; Carbohydrate: 87g; Fiber: 9g; Protein: 13g

Spiced Cauliflower and Potatoes

Bring a bold new bravado to slow cooking with Thai green chiles, an intensely hot pepper available in Asian markets. Slow cooking the peppers for a long period of time is the secret to coaxing the uniquely satisfying combination of hot and flavor out of them.

Preparation time: 30 minutes
Cooking time: 3 hours (LOW)

Ingredients

1 large head cauliflower cut into 1-inch florets (about 6 cups)
2 large potatoes, chopped and peeled (about 2 cups)
1 medium white or red onion, coarsely chopped (about 1/2 cup)
1 medium tomato, chopped (about 1/2 cup) (optional)
3 to 4 Thai, serrano, or cayenne chile peppers, stems removed, seeded (if desired), and chopped or sliced lengthwise *
3 tablespoons vegetable or canola oil
3 cloves garlic, minced
1 2-inch piece of fresh ginger, peeled and grated
1 tablespoon cumin seeds
1 tablespoon ground ancho chile pepper or chili powder
1 tablespoon garam masala
1 teaspoon ground turmeric
1 teaspoon salt
1 tablespoon snipped fresh cilantro
Roti ** (optional)

Directions

Combine all ingredients except the fresh cilantro and optional Roti in a 4 to 5 quart slow cooker.

Cover and cook on LOW for 3 hours, stirring once or twice early in the cooking.

Gently stir in the cilantro.

Serve with Roti if desired.

Makes 10 servings.

* Tip: Fresh chile peppers contain volatile oils that can burn your skin and eyes. Avoid direct contact with them as much as possible. Wear disposable plastic or rubber gloves when working with fresh chiles. If you do touch the chiles with your bare hands, wash your hands and nails thoroughly with soap and warm water.

** Tip: Roti is an unleavened Indian bread.

Per Serving

Calories: 95; Fat: 5g; Cholesterol: 0mg; Sodium: 264mg; Carbohydrate: 13g; Fiber: 3g; Protein: 3g

Black Bean Enchilada Casserole

Serve this meatless main dish with a salad of shredded lettuce topped with guacamole and a lime wedge.

Preparation time: 30 minutes
Cooking time: 3-1/2 hours (LOW)

Ingredients

2 tablespoons vegetable oil
1-1/2 cups chopped onion
3 garlic cloves, minced
1 teaspoon ground cumin
1/2 teaspoon salt
1/2 teaspoon ground coriander
1/8 teaspoon ground red pepper
2 cans (15-ounce, each) black beans, rinsed and drained
1 can (11-ounce) corn with red and green bell peppers, drained
1 can (4-1/2-ounce) chopped green chilies, drained
2 tablespoons chopped fresh cilantro
9 6-inch corn tortillas
2-1/2 cups shredded Mexican cheese blend
1 can (10-ounce) enchilada sauce
Sour cream (optional)
Chopped fresh cilantro (optional)

Directions

Heat the vegetable oil in a large skillet over medium heat. Add the onion and garlic and sauté for 5 minutes or until tender. Stir in the cumin, salt, coriander, and red pepper. Stir in the black beans, corn with red and green bell peppers, green chilies and 2 tablespoons of cilantro.

Place 3 tortillas in a lightly greased 4 quart slow cooker and top with half of the bean mixture, 3/4 cup of Mexican cheese blend, and half of the enchilada sauce. Repeat the layer once, and top with the remaining 3 tortillas. Sprinkle with the remaining 1 cup of cheese

Cover and cook on low for 3-1/2 hours.

Serve garnished with sour cream and cilantro, if desired.

Makes 10 to 12 servings.

Per Serving

Calories: 193; Fat: 10g; Cholesterol: 18mg; Sodium: 687mg; Carbohydrate: 19g; Fiber: 4g; Protein: 8g

Curried Vegetables

If you know someone who does not like to eat vegetables, then this meal might just change their mind! Enjoy this simple and healthy vegetable medley simmered in a simple coconut curry.

Preparation time: 15 minutes
Cooking time: 6 hours (LOW) or 3 hours (HIGH), plus 15 minutes (LOW)

Ingredients

1 tablespoon olive oil
2 cups sliced carrots, cut 1 to 1-1/4 inches thick
1 onion, sliced thinly
3 cloves garlic, minced
2 tablespoon curry powder
1-1/2 teaspoon cayenne pepper
1-1/2 teaspoon turmeric
5 red potatoes quartered
10 ounces green beans (fresh or frozen)
1 cup tomatoes, diced
3 cups chickpeas, drained and rinsed
2 cups vegetable broth
1-1/2 cups frozen peas
1-1/2 cup coconut milk

Directions

Heat the olive oil in a pan and add the carrots and onions and sauté for 3 to 4 minutes.

Add the garlic, curry powder, cayenne pepper and turmeric and continue to cook for an additional 2 minutes, or until the spices become fragrant.

Transfer the mixture to a 3-1/2 or 4 quart slow cooker.

Add the red potatoes, green beans, tomatoes, chickpeas and vegetable broth to the slow cooker.

Cook on LOW for 6 hours or on HIGH for 3 hours.

Add the frozen peas and coconut milk and cook for an additional 15 minutes on LOW.

Makes 8 servings.

Per Serving

Calories: 180; Fat: 3g; Cholesterol: 0mg; Sodium: 393mg; Carbohydrate: 30g; Fiber: 8g; Protein: 7g

Vegetarian Spaghetti Sauce

This sauce tastes so good everyone will think that you have been slaving over the stove for hours. Serve over hot rice, pasta of your choice or it can be used as a base for chili.

Preparation time: 20 minutes
Cooking time: 10 to 12 hours (LOW) or 5 to 6 hours (HIGH)

Ingredients

5 plum tomatoes, cut into wedges
2 cups dried soybeans
1 large onion, diced
1 pound okra chopped (fresh or frozen)
1 cup black olives, pitted
1 cup green olives, pitted
1 can (14-ounce) tomato paste
3 cans (14-ounce, each) diced tomatoes
1 cup red wine
1 cup grated Parmesan cheese *
1/4 cup olive oil
1 can (11-ounce) corn, drained
3 tablespoons dried oregano
3 tablespoons dried basil
5 tablespoons Italian seasoning
Salt and red pepper flakes to season
24 ounces spaghetti pasta, cooked, hot (or your choice of pasta)
Parmesan cheese (optional) *

* Since Parmesan cheese is made with rennet, which is derived from the stomach of slaughtered cows, some vegetarians may choose not to utilize it. You may instead substitute the Parmesan cheese for nutritional yeast.

Directions

Soak the soybeans for at least 8 hours or overnight.

Combine all the ingredients except the pasta in a 5 to 6 quart slow cooker and cook for 10 to 12 hours on LOW or 5 to 6 hours on HIGH.

Serve the sauce over the hot cooked pasta and sprinkle with Parmesan cheese (or nutritional yeast), if desired.

Makes 12 servings.

Per Serving

Calories: 385; Fat: 18g; Cholesterol: 6mg; Sodium: 1,347mg; Carbohydrate: 11g; Fiber: 9g; Protein: 2g

Winter Vegetable Risotto

Arborio rice is a short-grain rice grown in the Arborio region of Italy. It's especially suited for making risotto, as it cooks to a wonderful creaminess.

Preparation Time: 20 minutes
Cooking Time: 1-1/4 hours (HIGH)

Ingredients

3 cups vegetable broth
1 small onion, chopped
3 cloves garlic, minced
1 cup sliced cremini or white mushrooms
1 teaspoon dried rosemary
1 teaspoon thyme leaves
1-1/2 cups Arborio rice
1 cup small Brussels sprouts
1 cup sweet potatoes, peeled and cubed
1/4 cup grated Parmesan cheese (about 1-ounce) *
Salt and pepper to taste

* Since Parmesan cheese is made with rennet, which is derived from the stomach of slaughtered cows, some vegetarians may choose not to utilize it. You may instead substitute the Parmesan cheese for nutritional yeast.

Directions

Heat the vegetable broth in a small saucepan and pour into 3-1/2 or 4 quart slow cooker.

Add the remaining ingredients, except for the Parmesan cheese, salt, and pepper.

Cover and cook on HIGH for 1-1/4 hours, or until the rice is al dente and the liquid is almost absorbed (watch carefully and do not let the rice overcook).

Stir in the Parmesan cheese (or nutritional yeast) and season to taste with salt and pepper.

Makes 4 entrée size servings.

Summer Vegetable Risotto: Make the recipe as above, substituting 4 sliced green onions for the chopped onion, 1 cup chopped plum tomatoes for the mushrooms, and 3/4 cup each cubed zucchini and summer yellow squash for the Brussels sprouts and sweet potatoes.

Per Serving

Calories: 384; Fat: 8g; Cholesterol: 5mg; Sodium: 153mg; Carbohydrate: 77g; Fiber: 8g; Protein: 11g

Ultimate Macaroni and Cheese

A combination of four cheeses makes this the best macaroni and cheese ever!

Preparation time: 15 minutes
Cooking time: 3 hours (LOW)

Ingredients

3 cups whole milk
1/3 cup all-purpose flour
1 cup shredded reduced-fat mozzarella cheese (about 4-ounces)
1 cup shredded cheddar cheese (about 4-ounces)
1 cup crumbled blue cheese (about 4-ounces)
1/2 cup Parmesan cheese, divided (about 2-ounces) *
1 pound ziti or penne pasta, cooked al dente

* *Since Parmesan cheese is made with rennet, which is derived from the stomach of slaughtered cows, some vegetarians may choose not to utilize it. You may instead substitute the Parmesan cheese for nutritional yeast.*

Directions

Generously coat the bottom and sides of a 6 quart slow cooker.

Mix the milk and flour until smooth in a large bowl and add the remaining ingredients, except for 1/4 cup of the Parmesan cheese (or nutritional yeast) and ziti.

Mix in the ziti and spoon into the slow cooker. Sprinkle the remaining 1/4 cup of Parmesan cheese (or nutritional yeast).

Cover and cook on LOW for 3 hours.

Makes 8 servings.

Per Serving

Calories: 439; Fat: 31g; Cholesterol: 44mg; Sodium: 673mg; Carbohydrate: 52g; Fiber: 3g; Protein: 22g

Tropical Stuffed Cabbage Rolls

If you love cabbage rolls then you should try this slow cooked, meatless version. Enjoy the nice tropical flavors that emanate from the combination of orzo, black beans, pineapple preserves and curry.

Preparation time: 30 minutes
Cooking time: 7 to 9 hours (LOW)

Ingredients

1 can (14-ounce) light unsweetened coconut milk (not creamed coconut)
1/2 cup pineapple preserves
8 large cabbage leaves
1 cup cooked orzo or rosa marina pasta
1 medium onion, chopped (about 1/2 cup)
1/3 cup raisins
1/3 cup cashews pieces
2 teaspoons curry powder
1/2 teaspoon garlic onion
1 can (15-ounce) black beans drained, rinsed

Directions

Spray a 3 to 4 quart slow cooker with cooking spray.

Mix the coconut milk and pineapple preserves in a small bowl.

Spread a 1/2 cup of the coconut milk and preserve mixture in the bottom of the slow cooker.

Cover the cabbage leaves with boiling water in a large bowl. Cover the bowl and let stand for approximately 10 minutes or until the cabbage leaves are limp. Drain.

Mix the pasta, onion, raisins, cashews, curry powder, garlic salt and black beans in a medium bowl.

Place about 1/3 cup of the pasta mixture at the stem end of each cabbage leaf. Roll the leaf around the pasta mixture, tucking in the sides.

Place as many cabbage rolls, seam sides down, that will comfortably fit in one layer in the slow cooker. Cover with 1/3 cup of the coconut milk mixture. Layer with the remaining cabbage rolls and pour the remaining coconut milk mixture over the top.

Cover and cook on LOW for 7 to 9 hours.

With a spatula, carefully remove the cabbage rolls from the slow cooker.

Makes 4 servings.

Per Serving

Calories: 670; Fat: 27g; Cholesterol: 2mg; Sodium: 620mg; Carbohydrate: 91g; Fiber: 16g; Protein: 16g

Desserts

RECIPES

Gingerbread Pudding Cake 88
Orange-Caramel Pudding Cake 90
Mixed Berry Pudding Cake 92
Fruit Compote 94
Cinnamon Apples 95
Champagne Poached Pears..97
Dutch Apple Pudding Cake..99
Old Fashioned Rice Pudding 101
Triple-Chocolate Peanut Butter Pudding Cake 103
Tropical Apricot Crisp 105
Hot Fudge Sundae Cake 107
Blackberry Dumplings..109
Easy Cherry Cobbler 111

Gingerbread Pudding Cake

This is an easy to make and comforting slow cooker dessert that smells amazing while it is cooking.

Preparation time: 15 minutes
Cooking time: 2 hours (HIGH)
Cooling time: 45 minutes

Ingredients

Non-stick cooking spray
1 package (14-1/2-ounces) gingerbread mix
1/2 cup milk
1/2 cup raisins
2-1/4 cups water
3/4 cup packed brown sugar
3/4 cup butter
Vanilla ice cream or sweetened whipped cream (optional)

Directions

Lightly coat the inside of a 3-1/2 or 4 quart slow cooker with the cooking spray and set aside.

Stir together the gingerbread mix and milk in a small bowl until moistened.

Stir in the raisins (the batter will be thick).

Spread the batter evenly in the prepared slow cooker.

In a medium saucepan, combine the water, brown sugar, and the butter. Bring to a boil and then carefully pour the mixture over the batter in the slow cooker.

Cover and cook on HIGH for 2 hours (the center may appear moist but will firm as it stands).

Remove the liner from the cooker, if possible, or turn off the slow cooker.

Let stand uncovered for 45 minutes to cool slightly.

To serve, spoon the warm pudding cake into dessert dishes and, if desired, serve with ice cream.

Makes 8 servings.

Per Serving

Calories: 501; Fat: 24g; Cholesterol: 50mg; Sodium: 548mg; Carbohydrate: 70g; Fiber: 1g; Protein: 4g

Orange-Caramel Pudding Cake

This is a classic combination of moist, tender cake and crunchy chopped pecans smothered in a decadently rich orange-caramel sauce.

Preparation time: 25 minutes
Cooking time: 4-1/2 to 5 hours (LOW)
Cooling time: 45 minutes

Ingredients:

Non-stick cooking spray
1 cup all-purpose flour
1/3 cup granulated sugar
1 teaspoon baking powder
1/2 teaspoon ground cinnamon
1/4 teaspoon salt
1/2 cup milk
2 tablespoons butter, melted
1/2 cup chopped pecans
1/4 cup dried currants or raisins
3/4 cup water
1/2 teaspoon finely shredded orange peel
3/4 cup orange juice
2/3 cup packed brown sugar
1 tablespoon butter
Caramel-flavor ice cream topping
Chopped pecans
Sweetened whipped cream (optional)

Directions

Lightly coat the inside of a 3-1/2 or 4 quart slow cooker with the cooking spray and set aside.

Stir together the flour, granulated sugar, baking powder, cinnamon, and salt in a medium bowl. Stir in the milk and melted butter. Stir in the 1/2 cup pecans and 1/4 cup currants or raisins.

Spread the batter in the prepared slow cooker.

In a medium saucepan, combine the water, orange peel, orange juice, brown sugar, and 1 tablespoon of butter. Bring to a boil, stirring to dissolve the brown sugar then reduce the heat. Boil gently, uncovered for 2 minutes then carefully pour over the mixture in the slow cooker.

Cover and cook on LOW for 4-1/2 to 5 hours.

Remove the liner from the slow cooker, if possible, or turn off the cooker.

Let stand uncovered for 45 minutes to cool slightly.

To serve, spoon the cake into dishes and top with caramel topping, pecans, and if desired, whipped cream.

Makes 6 to 8 servings.

Per Serving

Calories: 390; Fat: 15g; Cholesterol: 25mg; Sodium: 255mg; Carbohydrate: 61g; Fiber: 2g; Protein: 5g

Mixed Berry Pudding Cake

This is a delightfully delicious, sweet tooth indulging fruit dessert that is slow cooked with a hint of cinnamon and vanilla.

Preparation time: 20 minutes
Cooking time: 2-1/2 to 3 hours (HIGH)
Cooling time: 1 hour

Ingredients

Nonstick cooking spray
1-1/2 cups loose-pack frozen blueberries
1-1/2 cups loose-pack frozen red raspberries
1/2 cup fresh cranberries
1 cup all-purpose flour
2/3 cup sugar
1-1/2 teaspoons baking powder
1/2 teaspoon ground cinnamon
1/4 teaspoon salt
1/2 cup milk
2 tablespoons butter, melted
1 teaspoon vanilla
3/4 cup boiling water
1/3 cup sugar
1/2 cup sliced almonds, toasted (optional)

Directions

Lightly coat a 3-1/2 or 4 quart slow cooker with non-stick cooking spray.

Combine the frozen blueberries, frozen raspberries, and fresh cranberries in the prepared slow cooker and set aside.

Combine the flour, the 2/3 cup sugar, the baking powder, cinnamon, and salt in a medium bowl. Stir in the milk melted butter, and vanilla just until combined.

Spoon and carefully spread the batter over the berries in the slow cooker.

Combine the boiling water and the 1/3 cup sugar in a small bowl and stir to dissolve the sugar. Pour evenly over the mixture in the slow cooker.

Cover and cook on HIGH for 2-1/2 to 3 hours or until a toothpick inserted near the center of the cake comes out clean.

Remove the slow cooker liner if possible, or turn the slow cooker off.

Cool, uncovered, for 1 hour.

To serve, spoon the warm pudding cake into dessert dishes and sprinkle each serving with almonds, if desired

Makes 8 servings.

Per Serving

Calories: 260; Fat: 8g; Cholesterol: 9mg; Sodium: 146mg; Carbohydrate: 45g; Fiber: 4g; Protein: 4g

Fruit Compote

This is a quick and very easy to make slow cooker fruit compote that will come in handy on those days when you are struggling to get all you servings of fruit.

Preparation time: 15 minutes
Cooking time: 8 to 10 hours (LOW) or 4 to 5 hours (HIGH)

Ingredients

2 cans (10-ounce, each) pineapple chunks, undrained
1 package (15-ounces) golden raisins or dried mixed apples, peaches, and apricots
1 cup low-fat granola
1 cup water
1 teaspoon apple pie spice

Directions

Put the pineapple chunks, granola, dried fruit, water, and apple pie spice in the slow cooker and stir to combine.

Cover and cook on LOW for 8 to 10 hours or on HIGH for 4 to 5 hours, or until the flavors have melded and the mixture has become very thick. Stir every 2 hours, adding water as needed.

Makes 10 servings.

Per Serving

Calories: 290; Fat: 1g; Cholesterol: 0mg; Sodium: 40mg; Carbohydrate: 65g; Fiber: 4g; Protein: 3g

Cinnamon Apples

Serve these sweet apples alone, or spoon them over vanilla ice cream or pound cake for dessert.

Preparation time: 15 minutes
Cooking time: 6 hours (LOW)

Ingredients

6 medium-size Granny Smith apples, peeled and cut into eights
1 tablespoons lemon juice
1/2 cup firmly packed dark brown sugar
1/2 cup chopped walnuts
1/2 cup maple syrup
1/4 cup sweetened dried cranberries
1/4 cup butter, melted
2 teaspoons ground cinnamon
2 tablespoons water
1 tablespoon cornstarch

Directions

Combine the apples and lemon juice in a 4 quart slow cooker and toss well to coat. Add the brown sugar, and the next 5 ingredients and combine well.

Cover and cook on LOW for 3 hours.

Stir together the water and cornstarch in a small bowl and stir into the apples.

Cover and cook on LOW for 3 more hours or until the apples are tender.

Makes 10 to 12 servings.

Per Serving

Calories: 192; Fat: 8g; Cholesterol: 11mg; Sodium: 35mg; Carbohydrate: 32g; Fiber: 4g; Protein: 1g

Champagne Poached Pears

This savory Champagne poached pear recipe is a perfect dessert option for a cold winter night or an elegant brunch dish.

Preparation time: 20 minutes
Cooking time: 3 to 4 hours (HIGH)
Cooling time: 30 minutes

Ingredients

4 whole Comice or Anjou pears, with stems attached
Finely grated zest and strained juice of 1 large lemon
3 cups Champagne, plus more if needed
1 cup granulated sugar

Directions

With a sharp knife or grapefruit spoon, and working from the bottom of each pear, dig out the core and seeds. Peel the pears, leaving the stems in place.

Place the whole pears, standing upright in 3 quart slow cooker.

Stir together the lemon zest and juice, Champagne, and sugar. Pour the mixture over the pears in the slow cooker.

Cover and cook on HIGH for 3 to 4 hours, or until the pears are tender.

Turn off the slow cooked and allow the pears to cool in the syrup.

To serve, place a pear in each of 4 bowls and spoon on some syrup.

Makes 4 servings.

Per Serving

Calories: 230; Fat: 0g; Cholesterol: 0mg; Sodium: 0mg; Carbohydrate: 51g; Fiber: 7g; Protein: 1g

Dutch Apple Pudding Cake

This is a delicious take on an amazing cake, and the convenience of the slow cooker make this luscious cake recipe even easier to make.

Preparation time: 25 minutes
Cooking time: 2 to 2-1/2 hours (HIGH)
Cooling time: 30 to 45 minutes

Ingredients

Nonstick cooking spray
1 can (20 or 21-ounce) apple pie filling
1/2 cup dried cherries, dried cranberries, or raisins
1 cup all-purpose flour
1/4 cup granulated sugar
1 teaspoon baking powder
1/4 teaspoon salt
1/2 cup milk
2 tablespoons butter, melted
1/2 cup chopped walnuts, toasted
1-1/4 cups apple juice
1/3 cup packed brown sugar
1 tablespoon butter
1 recipe Sweetened Whipped Cream (optional)
Chopped walnuts, toasted (optional)

Directions

Lightly coat a 3-1/2 or 4 quart slow cooker with cooking spray and set aside.

Bring the apple pie filling to boiling in a small saucepan and stir in the cherries. Transfer the apple mixture to the prepared slow cooker.

Stir together the flour, granulated sugar, baking powder, and salt in a medium bowl. Add the milk and melted butter and stir just until combined. Stir in the 1/2 cup walnuts. Pour and evenly spread the batter over the apple mixture in the slow cooker.

In the same saucepan, combine the apple juice, brown sugar, and the 1 tablespoon of butter and bring to a boil. Boil gently, uncovered, for 2 minutes. Carefully pour the apple juice mixture over the mixture in the slow cooker.

Cover and cook on HIGH for 2 to 2-1/2 hours or until a wooden toothpick inserted near the center of the cake comes out clean.

Remove the liner from the cooker if possible, or turn off the slow cooker.

Cool, uncovered for 30 to 45 minutes.

To serve, spoon the warm cake and its sauce into dessert dishes and, if desired, top each serving with Sweetened Whipped Cream and the additional walnuts.

Makes 6 to 8 servings.

Sweetened Whipped Cream: Chill a small bowl and the beaters of an electric mixer. In the chilled bowl, combine 1/2 cup whipping cream and 2 teaspoons brown sugar. Beat with the electric mixer on medium speed until soft peaks form.

Per Serving

Calories: 435; Fat: 13g; Cholesterol: 18mg; Sodium: 284mg; Carbohydrate: 77g; Fiber: 3g; Protein: 5g

Old Fashioned Rice Pudding

No stirring or watching needed when rice pudding is made in the slow cooker. This version is flecked with raisins, dried cranberries, and/or dried cherries for a homey, comforting dessert.

Preparation time: 10 minutes
Cooking time: 2 to 3 hours (LOW)

Ingredients

Nonstick cooking spray
4 cups cooked rice
1 can (12-ounce) evaporated milk
1 cup milk
1/3 cup sugar
1/4 cup water
1 cup raisins, dried cranberries, and/or dried cherries
3 tablespoons butter softened
1 tablespoon vanilla or vanilla bean paste
1 teaspoon ground cinnamon

Directions

Lightly coat the inside of a 3-1/2 or 4 quart slow cooker with the cooking spray and set aside.

Combine the cooked rice, evaporated milk, milk, sugar, and the water in a large bowl. Stir in the raisins, butter, vanilla, and the cinnamon.

Transfer the mixture to the prepared slow cooker.

Cover and cook on LOW for 2 to 3 hours.

Stir gently before serving.

Makes 12 to 14 servings.

Per Serving

Calories: 204; Fat: 6g; Cholesterol: 18mg; Sodium: 73mg; Carbohydrate: 34g; Fiber: 1g; Protein: 4g

Triple-Chocolate Peanut Butter Pudding Cake

An amazing dessert made in your slow cooker that is meant to be served warm. You can even add a scoop of vanilla ice cream and serve a la mode!

Preparation time: 20 minutes
Cooking time: 2 to 2-1/2 hours (HIGH)
Cooling time: 30 to 40 minutes

Ingredients

Non-stick cooking spray
1 cup all-purpose flour
1/3 cup sugar
2 tablespoons unsweetened cocoa powder
1-1/2 teaspoons baking powder
1/2 cup chocolate milk or regular milk
2 tablespoons vegetable oil
2 teaspoons vanilla
1/2 cup peanut butter-flavor pieces
1/2 cup semisweet chocolate pieces
1/2 cup chopped peanuts
3/4 cup sugar
2 tablespoons unsweetened cocoa powder
1-1/2 cups boiling water
Vanilla ice cream (optional)
Chocolate bar pieces (optional)

Directions

Lightly coat the inside of a 3-1/2 or 4 quart slow cooker with the cooking spray and set aside.

Stir together the flour, the 1/3 cup sugar, 2 tablespoons cocoa powder, and baking powder in a medium bowl. Add the chocolate milk, vegetable oil, and vanilla and stir just until moistened.

Stir in the peanut butter pieces, chocolate pieces, and chopped peanuts.

Spread the batter evenly in the prepared slow cooker.

In another medium bowl, combine the 3/4 cup sugar and 2 tablespoons cocoa powder. Gradually stir in the boiling water. Carefully pour the cocoa mixture over the batter in the cooker.

Cover and cook on HIGH for 2 to 2-1/2 hours or until a toothpick inserted into the center of the cake comes out clean.

Remove the liner from the slow cooker, if possible, or turn the cooker off.

Let stand uncovered for 30 to 40 minutes to cool slightly.

To serve, spoon the pudding cake into dessert dishes and, if desired, top with ice cream and/or chocolate bar pieces.

Makes 8 servings.

Per Serving

Calories: 372; Fat: 15g; Cholesterol: 3mg; Sodium: 125mg; Carbohydrate: 52g; Fiber: 3g; Protein: 5g

Tropical Apricot Crisp

The toasted coconut and crunchy granola topping takes your palate to warmer climates.

Preparation time: 10 minutes
Cooking time: 2-1/2 hours (LOW)
Cooling time: 30 minutes

Ingredients

Non-stick cooking spray
2 cans (21-ounce, each) apricot pie filling
1 package (7-ounces) tropical blend mixed dried fruit bits
1 cup granola
1/3 cup coconut, toasted *
2 cups vanilla ice cream (optional)
Honey (optional)

Directions

Lightly coat the inside of a 3-1/2 or 4 quart slow cooker with the cooking spray.

Combine the apricot pie filling and mixed dried fruit bits in the prepared slow cooker

Cover and cook on LOW for 2-1/2 hours.

Remove the liner from the slow cooker, if possible, or turn the cooker off.

In a small bowl, combine the granola and toasted coconut. Sprinkle over the mixture in the slow cooker.

Let stand uncovered for about 30 minutes to cool slightly.

Serve by spooning the warm apricot mixture into dessert dishes and, if desired, topping with scoops of ice cream and/or drizzled with honey.

Makes 6 servings.

*** Tip:** To toast coconut, preheat the oven to 350ºF. Spread the coconut in a shallow baking pan and bake for 5 to 10 minutes or until golden brown, watching closely to avoid burning and shaking the pan once or twice.

Per Serving

Calories: 587; Fat: 13g; Cholesterol: 45mg; Sodium: 144mg; Carbohydrate: 109g; Fiber: 7g; Protein: 6g

Hot Fudge Sundae Cake

For a special treat, add 1/3 cup halved maraschino cherries with the nuts. Top with a scoop of your favorite ice cream. Tuck a long-stemmed maraschino cherry on top of each servings to make this the best ever sundae cake.

Preparation time: 15 minutes
Cooking time: 2 to 2-1/2 hours (HIGH)
Cooling time: 30 to 40 minutes

Ingredients

1 cup all-purpose flour
1/2 cup granulated sugar
2 tablespoons baking cocoa
2 tablespoons baking powder
1/2 teaspoon salt
1/2 cup milk
2 tablespoons vegetable oil
1 teaspoon vanilla
1/2 cup chopped nuts
3/4 cup packed brown sugar
1/4 cup baking cocoa
1-1/2 cups hot water

Directions

Spray the inside of a 2 to 3-1/2 quart slow cooker with cooking spray.

Mix the all-purpose flour, granulated sugar, 2 tablespoons cocoa, the baking powder and salt in a medium bowl. Stir in the milk, vegetable oil and vanilla until smooth. Stir in the nuts.

Spread the batter evenly in the bottom of the slow cooker.

Mix the brown sugar and 1/4 cup cocoa in a small bowl. Stir in the hot water until smooth and pour evenly over the batter in the slow cooker.

Cover and cook on HIGH for 2 to 2-1/2 hours or until a toothpick inserted in the center comes out clean.

Turn off the cooker and let the cake stand uncovered for 30 to 40 minutes to cool slightly before serving.

Spoon the warm cake into dessert dishes and spoon the sauce over top.

Makes 6 servings

Per Serving

Calories: 380; Fat: 12g; Cholesterol: 0mg; Sodium: 380mg; Carbohydrate: 66g; Fiber: 3g; Protein: 5g

Blackberry Dumplings

You can easily modify this recipe by adding your favorite frozen berries. Feel free to try blueberries, strawberries, raspberries or any combination of two or even all three. But remember, if using frozen berries, be sure to buy the bag of berries that are not frozen in syrup.

Preparation time: 10 minutes
Cooking time: 3 to 4 hours (LOW) or 1-1/2 to 2 hours (HIGH), plus 20 to 25 minutes (HIGH)

Ingredients

1 package (14-ounces) frozen blackberries (about 3 cups), thawed and drained
1/3 cup sugar
1/3 cup water
1 teaspoon lemon juice
1 cup Bisquick Original baking mix
2 tablespoons sugar
1/3 cup milk
Ground cinnamon
Whipping (heavy) cream or vanilla ice cream (optional)

Directions

Mix the blackberries, 1/3 cup sugar, water, and lemon juice in a 3-1/2 or 4 quart slow cooker.

Cover and cook on LOW for 3 to 4 hours or on HIGH for 1-1/2 to 2 hours, or until the mixture is boiling.

Mix the baking mix and 2 tablespoons sugar in a small bowl. Stir in the milk just until the dry ingredients are moistened.

Drop the dough by 6 spoonfuls onto the hot berry mixture and sprinkle with the cinnamon.

Cover and cook on HIGH for an additional 20 to 25 minutes or until a toothpick inserted in the center of the dumplings comes out clean.

Serve by spooning the dumplings into a dessert dish and spoon the berry mixture over top. Top with whipping cream, if desired.

Makes 6 servings.

Per Serving

Calories: 165; Fat: 3g; Cholesterol: 0mg; Sodium: 290mg; Carbohydrate: 37g; Fiber: 4g; Protein: 2g

Easy Cherry Cobbler

Pass a pitcher of heavy whipping cream, half-and-half or eggnog, when it is available, to pour over the bowls of warm cobbler. Sprinkle a little ground cinnamon or nutmeg on top for just a hint of spiciness.

Preparation time: 10 minutes
Cooking time: 1-1/2 to 2 hours (HIGH)

Ingredients

1 can (21-ounce) cherry pie filling
1 cup all-purpose flour
1/4 cup sugar
1/4 cup margarine or butter, melted
1/2 cup milk
1-1/2 teaspoons baking powder
1/2 teaspoon almond extract
1/4 teaspoon salt

Directions

Spray the inside of a 2 to 3-1/2 quart slow cooker with cooking spray.

Pour the cherry pie filling into the slow cooker.

Beat the remaining ingredients with a spoon until smooth. Spread the batter over the pie filling.

Cover and cook on HIGH for 1-1/2 to 2 hours or until a toothpick inserted in the center comes out clean

Makes 6 servings.

Per Serving

Calories: 270; Fat: 8g; Cholesterol: 0mg; Sodium: 330mg; Carbohydrate: 49g; Fiber: 2g; Protein: 3g

Fondues

RECIPES

Cheese Fondue 113
Butterscotch Fondue 115
S'More Fondue 116
Candy Bar Fondue 117
Mexican Fondue 119
Pizza Fondue 121

Cheese Fondue

Combining cheese and wine is not only delicious but also extremely savvy. The addition of the wine contributes two essential elements for a smooth fondue: 1) liquid, which keeps the casein proteins moist and dilute, and 2) tartaric acid, which pulls the cross-linking calcium off of the casein proteins and binds tightly to it, leaving them glue-less and happily separate.

Preparation time: 5 minutes
Cooking time: 2 hours (HIGH), plus 2 hours (LOW)

Ingredients

2-1/2 cups dry white wine
3 garlic cloves
16 ounces of Gruyere cheese, grated
1 pound Swiss cheese, grated
3 tablespoons flour
3 tablespoons kirsch
1/4 teaspoon ground nutmeg

Directions

In a saucepan, simmer the dry white wine and the garlic.

Mix all the ingredients in 3-1/2 or 4 quart slow cooker.

Cover and cook on HIGH for 2 hours.

Sprinkle with the ground nutmeg, cover, and cook for another 2 hours on LOW.

Stir the fondue until smooth and serve with French bread cubes, spearing the bread and dipping it into the fondue.

If necessary, cover the fondue and hold in the slow cooker on LOW setting for up to 2 hours, stirring occasionally.

Makes about 15 servings.

Per 1/4 cup (without dippers)

Calories: 279; Fat: 18g; Cholesterol: 61mg; Sodium: 162mg; Carbohydrate: 4g; Fiber: 0g; Protein: 17g

Butterscotch Fondue

The combination of brown sugar, sweetened condensed milk and corn syrup has lovely flavor. Use it to cap off a meal...or serve it as a sweet snack.

Preparation time: 10 minutes
Cooking time: 1 to 2 hours (LOW)

Ingredients

2 cans (14-ounce, each) sweetened condensed milk
2 cups packed brown sugar
1 cup butter, melted
2/3 cup light-color corn syrup
1 teaspoon vanilla
1/4 cup rum or milk
1/4 cup milk
Assorted dippers (such as apple slices, strawberries, orange sections, cookies, and/or cubed brownies)

Directions

In a 3-1/2 or 4 quart slow cooker, stir together the sweetened condensed milk, brown sugar, melted butter, corn syrup, and vanilla.

Cover and cook on LOW (do not use HIGH) for 1 to 2 hours. Whisk in the rum and milk until smooth.

Serve immediately or keep warm, covered, on WARM setting for up to 2 hours, stirring occasionally to keep from scorching.

Serve the fondue with dippers, swirling pieces as you dip.

Makes about 20 servings.

Per 1/4 cup (without dippers)

Calories: 318; Fat: 13g; Cholesterol: 38mg; Sodium: 127mg;
Carbohydrate: 48g; Fiber: 0g; Protein: 3g

S'More Fondue

Try this taste sensation as a beautiful dessert fondue!

Preparation time: 10 minutes
Cooking time: 1-1/2 to 2 hours (LOW)

Ingredients

15 ounces milk chocolate bar, chopped
1 package (10-ounces) large marshmallows
1/2 cup half-and-half or light cream
Assorted dippers (such as graham cracker snack sticks, halved graham cracker squares, and/or large marshmallows)

Directions

In a 3-1/2 quart slow cooker, stir together the chocolate, marshmallows, and half-and-half.

Cover and cook on LOW for 1-1/2 to 2 hours, stirring once during cooking.

Whisk until the mixture is smooth.

Serve immediately or keep warm, covered, on WARM or LOW setting for up to 2 hours, stirring occasionally.

Serve the fondue with dippers, swirling pieces as you dip.

Makes 16 servings.

Per 1/4 cup (without dippers)

Calories: 404; Fat: 19g; Cholesterol: 12mg; Sodium: 54mg;
Carbohydrate: 63g; Fiber: 3g; Protein: 4g

Candy Bar Fondue

Add an interactive touch to dessert by making fondue with melted chocolate candy bars.

Preparation time: 15 minutes
Cooking time: 2 to 2-1/2 hours (LOW)

Ingredients

4 1.76 ounce bars chocolate-coated nougat with almonds, chopped
1 7-ounce bar milk chocolate, chopped
1 7-ounce jar marshmallow crème
3/4 cup whipping cream, half-and-half, or light cream
1/4 cup finely chopped almonds, toasted
2 to 3 tablespoons almond or hazelnut liqueur (optional)
Assorted dippers (such as cubed pound cake and/or fruit chunks)
Finely chopped toasted almonds, toasted coconut, miniature semisweet chocolate pieces, multicolor candy sprinkles, and/or toffee pieces (optional)

Directions

In a 3-1/2 quart slow cooker, combine the nougat bars, milk chocolate bar, marshmallow crème, and whipping cream.

Cover and cook on LOW for 2 to 2-1/2 hours.

Stir until smooth.

Stir in the 1/4 cup almonds and, if desired, the liqueur.

If desired, transfer the chocolate mixture to a 1-1/2 quart slow cooker. Serve the fondue immediately or keep warm, covered, on WARM or LOW setting for up to 1 hour, stirring occasionally.

Serve the fondue with dippers, swirling pieces as you dip. If desired, dip into additional almonds, coconut, chocolate pieces, candy sprinkles, and/or toffee pieces to coat.

Makes 12 servings.

<u>Per tablespoon (without dippers)</u>

Calories: 294; Fat: 16g; Cholesterol: 25mg; Sodium: 55mg;
Carbohydrate: 34g; Fiber: 1g; Protein: 3g

Mexican Fondue

This simple to prepare Mexican fondue offers a nice combination of spices with 2 different types of cheese.

Preparation time: 20 minutes
Cooking time: 3 to 4 hours (LOW) or 1-1/2 to 2 hours (HIGH)

Ingredients

1 can (14-1/2-ounce) diced tomatoes, undrained
2/3 cup finely chopped onion
1/2 cup finely chopped roasted red sweet pepper
1 can (4-ounce) diced green chile peppers, undrained
3 cups cubed Monterey jack cheese with jalapeno peppers or regular Monterey Jack cheese (about 12-ounces)
3 cups cubed American cheese (about 12-ounces)
Assorted dippers (such as toasted cubed corn bread) *
Milk

Directions

In a 3-1/2 or 4 quart slow cooker, combine the tomatoes, onion, roasted sweet pepper, and chile peppers. Add the cheeses and toss gently to combine.

Cover and cook on LOW for 3 to 4 hours or on HIGH for 1-1/2 to 2 hours.

Serve immediately or keep warm, covered on WARM or LOW setting for up to 2 hours.

Serve the fondue with dippers, swirling pieces as you dip. If the fondue thickens, stir in a little milk.

Makes 36 servings.

* Tip: To toast the corn bread cubes, arrange them on a shallow baking pan. Bake in a 300°F oven for 10 to 15 minutes, stirring once or twice.

Per 3 tablespoons (without dippers)

Calories: 77; Fat: 6g; Cholesterol: 19mg; Sodium: 236mg; Carbohydrate: 1g; Fiber: 0g; Protein: 5g

Pizza Fondue

Make this delicious pizza flavored fondue recipe to please the pizza lovers in your family.

Preparation time: 10 minutes
Cooking time: 45 to 60 minutes (HIGH)

Ingredients

16 ounces American cheese, cut into cubes
8 ounces shredded mozzarella cheese
1 jar (28-ounces) tomato pasta sauce
1/2 cup dry red wine
1 loaf Italian bread, cut into 1-inch cubes, if desired

Directions

Spray the inside of a 3 or 4 quart slow cooker with cooking spray and add the American cheese, mozzarella cheese, tomato pasta sauce and red wine.

Cover and cook on HIGH for 45 to 60 minutes.

Stir until the cheese is smooth and scrape down the side of the slow cooker with a rubber spatula to help prevent the edge of the fondue from scorching.

Reduce the heat to LOW and serve the fondue with the Italian bread cubes and wooden picks or fondue forks for dipping.

The fondue will hold up to 4 hours.

Makes 45 servings.

Per serving (without dippers)

Calories: 70; Fat: 4g; Cholesterol: 10mg; Sodium: 250mg; Carbohydrate: 3g; Fiber: 0g; Protein: 4g

Potluck

RECIPES

Apple-Buttered Sweet Potatoes 123
Herbed Wild Rice 124
Cowboy Rice and Beans 126
California Vegetable Casserole 128
Lemon-Pesto New Potatoes 129
Cheesy Succotash 131
Saucy Green Beans and Potatoes 132
Cauliflower and Broccoli in Swiss Cheese Sauce 133
Western Beans 134
Creamy Corn and Roasted Red Peppers 135
Balsamic Root Vegetables 136
Smoky Scalloped Potatoes 137

Apple-Buttered Sweet Potatoes

No pumpkin pie spice on hand? Just mix together 3/4 teaspoon ground cinnamon, 1/4 teaspoon ground ginger, 1/4 teaspoon allspice, and 1/4 teaspoon nutmeg.

Preparation time: 15 minutes
Cooking time: 6 to 7 hours (LOW) or 3 to 3-1/2 hours (HIGH)

Ingredients

3 pounds sweet potatoes, peeled and cut into 1-inch pieces (about 8 cups)
2 medium Granny Smith or other tart cooking apples, cored and cut into wedges
1/2 cup dried cherries or dried cranberries (optional)
1 cup whipping cream
1 cup apple butter
1-1/2 teaspoons pumpkin pie spice

Directions

In a 3-1/2 or 4 quart slow cooker, combine the sweet potatoes, apples, and, if desired, dried cherries.

Combine the whipping cream, apple butter, and pumpkin pie spice in a medium bowl. Pour the apple butter mixture over the sweet potato mixture in the slow cooker and stir gently to combine.

Cover and cook on LOW for 6 to 7 hours or on HIGH for 3 to 3-1/2 hours.

Makes 10 servings.

Per Serving

Calories: 351; Fat: 9g; Cholesterol: 33mg; Sodium: 25mg; Carbohydrate: 65g; Fiber: 5g; Protein: 2g

Herbed Wild Rice

Toothsome wild rice cooked with carrots, mushrooms, onions, tomatoes, and a generous medley of herbs.

Preparation time: 20 minutes
Cooking time: 6 to 7 hours (LOW) or 3 to 3-1/2 hours (HIGH)

Ingredients

2 cups fresh button mushrooms, quartered
3 medium onions, chopped (about 1-1/2 cups)
1 cup cooked wild rice, rinsed and drained
1 cup cooked regular brown rice, rinsed and drained
2 medium carrots, sliced (about 1 cup)
1 tablespoon butter
4 cloves garlic, minced
1 teaspoon dried basil, crushed
1/2 teaspoon dried thyme, crushed
1/2 teaspoon dried rosemary, crushed
1/4 teaspoon ground black pepper
2 cans (14-ounce, each) vegetable broth
1 can (14-1/2-ounce) diced tomatoes, undrained

Directions

In a 3-1/2 or 4 quart slow cooker, combine the mushrooms, onions, wild rice, brown rice, carrots, butter, garlic, basil, thyme, rosemary, and black pepper. Stir in the vegetable broth and tomatoes.

Cover and cook on LOW for 6 to 7 hours or on HIGH for 3 to 3-1/2 hours.

Stir before serving.

Makes 12 to 14 servings.

Per Serving

Calories: 143; Fat: 2g; Cholesterol: 3mg; Sodium: 333mg; Carbohydrate: 28g; Fiber: 2g; Protein: 4g

Cowboy Rice and Beans

Chili beans and a jalapeno pepper gives this slow cooker version of a popular BBQ multi-bean bake its kick.

Preparation time: 15 minutes
Cooking time: 5 to 6 hours (LOW) or 2-1/2 to 3 hours (HIGH), plus 30 minutes (HIGH)

Ingredients

2 cans (15-ounce, each) chili beans in chili gravy
1 can (15-ounce) butter beans, rinsed and drained
1 can (15-ounce) black beans, rinsed and drained
1 large onion, chopped (about 1 cup)
1 medium green sweet pepper, chopped (about 3/4 cup)
1 medium red sweet pepper, chopped (about 3/4 cup)
1 medium fresh jalapeno chile pepper, seeded and finely chopped *
1 bottle (18-ounces) barbecue sauce
1 cup vegetable broth
1 cup uncooked instant brown rice

Directions

Combine the chili beans in chili gravy, drained butter beans, drained black beans, onion, green sweet pepper, red sweet pepper, and jalapeno chili pepper in a 5 to 6 quart slow cooker.

Stir in the barbecue sauce and vegetable broth.

Cover and cook on LOW for 5 to 6 hours or on HIGH for 2-1/2 to 3 hours.

If using the LOW setting, turn to HIGH and stir in the uncooked brown rice. Cover and cook for an additional 30 minutes or until the rice is tender.

Makes 12 servings.

* Tip: Chile peppers contain volatile oils that can burn your skin and eyes. Caution is advised and you should avoid direct contact with them as much as possible. Wear plastic or rubber gloves when working with chile peppers. If you do touch the peppers with your bare hands, immediately wash you hands and nails with soap and warm water.

Per Serving

Calories: 365; Fat: 3g; Cholesterol: 0mg; Sodium: 1,676mg; Carbohydrate: 68g; Fiber: 17g; Protein: 19g

California Vegetable Casserole

Here is an easy to make blend of vegetables, mushroom soup and rice that will please everyone at your next potluck!

Preparation time: 15 minutes
Cooking time: 4 to 5 hours (LOW) or 2 to 2-1/2 hours (HIGH)

Ingredients

1 package (16-ounces) frozen California-blend vegetables (cauliflower, broccoli, and carrots)
1 can (10-3/4-ounce) condensed cream of mushroom soup
1 cup uncooked instant white rice
1 cup milk
1/2 of a 15 ounce jar of process cheese dip (about 3/4 cup)
1 small onion, chopped (about 1/3 cup)
1/4 cup water
2 tablespoons butter, cut into small pieces

Directions

Place the frozen vegetables in a 3-1/2 or 4 quart slow cooker.

In a medium bowl, combine the cream of mushroom soup, white rice, milk, cheese dip, onion, water, and butter. Pour the mixture over the vegetables.

Cover and cook on LOW for 4 to 5 hours or on HIGH for 2 to 2-1/2 hours or until the vegetables and rice are tender.

Stir before serving.

Makes 8 servings.

Per Serving

Calories: 209; Fat: 12g; Cholesterol: 36mg; Sodium: 717mg;
Carbohydrate: 21g; Fiber: 2g; Protein: 6g

Lemon-Pesto New Potatoes

Lemon brightens the flavor of everything it touches. Here, it offers a balance to the rich and salty flavor notes of the pesto and Alfredo sauce.

Preparation time: 15 minutes
Cooking time: 5 to 6 hours (LOW)

Ingredients

3 pounds tiny new potatoes, halved or quartered (about 9 cups)
1 jar (15 to 16-ounces) Alfredo pasta sauce
1/3 cup basil pesto
1 tablespoon finely shredded lemon peel
1/4 to 1/2 teaspoon coarse ground black pepper
Finely shredded Parmesan cheese *

* *Since Parmesan cheese is made with rennet, which is derived from the stomach of slaughtered cows, some vegetarians may choose not to utilize it. You may instead substitute the Parmesan cheese for nutritional yeast.*

Directions

Place the potatoes in a 4 to 5 quart slow cooker.

For the sauce, combine the Alfredo sauce, pesto, lemon peel, and pepper in a small bowl. Pour the sauce over the potatoes, and stir to combine.

Cover and cook on LOW for 5 to 6 hours.

Using a slotted spoon, transfer the potatoes to a serving dish. Whisk the sauce in the cooker and pour over the potatoes. Sprinkle each serving with Parmesan cheese (or nutritional yeast).

Makes 10 to 12 servings.

Per Serving

Calories: 252; Fat: 14g; Cholesterol: 29mg; Sodium: 431mg; Carbohydrate: 26g; Fiber: 2g; Protein: 7g

Cheesy Succotash

Cream cheese and whole onions enhance this saucy Southern favorite.

Preparation time: 15 minutes
Cooking time: 7 to 8 hours (LOW) or 3-1/2 to 4 hours (HIGH)

Ingredients

2 packages (16-ounces, each) frozen whole kernel corn
1 package (16-ounce) frozen Lima beans
1 cup frozen small whole onions
1 can (10-3/4-ounce) condensed cream of celery soup
1 tub (8-ounces) cream cheese spread with chive and onion
1/4 cup water

Directions

In a 4 or 4-1/2 quart slow cooker, combine the corn, Lima beans, and onions.

In a medium bowl, stir together the soup, cream cheese, and the water. Stir the soup mixture into the vegetables.

Cover and cook on LOW for 7 to 8 hours or on HIGH for 3-1/2 to 4 hours.

Stir before serving.

Makes 12 servings.

Per Serving

Calories: 211; Fat: 8g; Cholesterol: 19mg; Sodium: 296mg;
Carbohydrate: 29g; Fiber: 4g; Protein: 6g

Saucy Green Beans and Potatoes

Potatoes and green beans achieve elegance in a mustard-dill sauce that owes its satiny texture to cream of celery soup.

Preparation time: 20 minutes
Cooking time: 6 to 8 hours (LOW) or 3 to 4 hours (HIGH)

Ingredients

2 pounds tiny new potatoes, halved or quartered
1 pound fresh green beans, trimmed and halved crosswise
1 can (10-3/4-ounce) condensed cream of celery soup
3/4 cup water
1/4 cup Dijon-style mustard
3/4 teaspoon dried dill weed

Directions

In a 3-1/2 or 4 quart slow cooker, combine the potatoes and green beans.

In a medium bowl, combine the soup, the water, mustard, and dill. Pour the soup mixture over the vegetables and stir gently to combine.

Cover and cook on LOW for 6 to 8 hours or on HIGH for 3 to 4 hours.

Stir gently before serving.

Makes 12 servings.

Per Serving

Calories: 95; Fat: 2g; Cholesterol: 1mg; Sodium: 313mg; Carbohydrate: 17g; Fiber: 3g; Protein: 3g

Cauliflower and Broccoli in Swiss Cheese Sauce

Swiss cheese and Alfredo sauce makes a rich blend, but it's the herbs that elevate this cheesy veggie dish to sublime.

Preparation time: 25 minutes
Cooking time: 6 to 7 hours (LOW) or 3 to 3-1/2 hours (HIGH)

Ingredients

4 cups broccoli florets
4 cups cauliflower florets
1 jar (15 to 16-ounces) Alfredo pasta sauce
1-1/2 cups torn process Swiss cheese (about 6-ounces)
1 large onion, chopped (about 1 cup)
1 teaspoon dried thyme, oregano, or basil, crushed
1/4 teaspoon ground black pepper
1/2 cup ranch-flavor sliced almonds (optional)

Directions

Combine all the ingredients except for the almonds in a 3-1/2 or 4 quart slow cooker.

Cover and cook on LOW for 6 to 7 hours or on HIGH for 3 to 3-1/2 hours.

Stir gently before serving and, if desired, sprinkle with almonds.

Makes 10 servings.

Per Serving

Calories: 177; Fat: 12g; Cholesterol: 37mg; Sodium: 573mg; Carbohydrate: 10g; Fiber: 2g; Protein: 8g

Western Beans

Potluck offerings don't come any easier than these well-seasoned beans. Dry mustard lends zip.

Preparation time: 15 minutes
Cooking time: 4 to 5 hours (LOW) or 2 to 2-1/2 hours (HIGH)

Ingredients

3 cans (28-ounce, each) vegetarian baked beans, drained
3/4 cup hot-style barbecue sauce
1 medium onion, chopped (about 1/2 cup)
1/3 cup packed brown sugar
1 tablespoon dry mustard

Directions

Combine all the ingredients in a 3-1/2 to 5 quart slow cooker.

Cover and cook on LOW for 4 to 5 hours or on HIGH for 2 to 2-1/2 hours.

Makes 12 servings.

Per Serving

Calories: 238; Fat: 1g; Cholesterol: 0mg; Sodium: 1,015mg;
Carbohydrate: 53g; Fiber: 10g; Protein: 10g

Creamy Corn and Roasted Red Peppers

A great combination of corn and roasted red sweet peppers topped with a delicious hollandaise sauce. This is sure to be a hit at the party!

Preparation time: 15 minutes
Cooking time: 6 to 8 hours (LOW) or 3 to 4 hours (HIGH)

Ingredients

3 packages (9 or 10-ounces, each) frozen whole kernel corn in light or regular butter sauce
1 jar (12-ounces) roasted red sweet peppers, drained and chopped (about 1 cup)
2 tablespoons thinly sliced green onion
2 cups milk
2 envelopes (0.9 to 1.25-ounce, each) hollandaise sauce mix
Green onion (optional)

Directions

Combine the frozen kernel corn, roasted red peppers, and the 2 tablespoons green onion in a 3-1/2 quart slow cooker.

In a small bowl, whisk the milk into the hollandaise sauce mix and add the sauce mixture to the slow cooker. Stir to combine.

Cover and cook on LOW for 6 to 8 hours or on HIGH for 3 to 4 hours.

Stir before serving and, if desired, garnish each serving with additional green onion.

Makes 8 servings.

Per Serving

Calories: 155; Fat: 2g; Cholesterol: 5mg; Sodium: 249mg; Carbohydrate: 32g; Fiber: 2g; Protein: 5g

Balsamic Root Vegetables

Balsamic vinegar's tangy, pungent sweetness is the perfect accent to earthy root vegetables.

Preparation time: 15 minutes
Cooking time: 9 to 11 hours (LOW) or 4-1/2 to 5-1/2 hours (HIGH)

Ingredients

1/2 of a 16 ounce package frozen small whole onion (2 cups)
5 baby red potatoes, halved
3 medium parsnips, peeled (if desired) and cut into 1 inch pieces
4 baby carrots cut into 1 to 2 inch pieces
1 cup vegetable broth
1/4 cup balsamic vinegar
2 tablespoons packed brown sugar
2 cloves garlic, minced
1/4 teaspoon salt
1/4 teaspoon ground black pepper

Directions

Combine all the ingredients in a 3-1/2 or 4 quart slow cooker.

Cover and cook on LOW for 9 to 11 hours or on HIGH for 4-1/2 to 5-1/2 hours.

Makes 8 servings.

Per Serving

Calories: 136; Fat: 1g; Cholesterol: 0mg; Sodium: 235mg; Carbohydrate: 32g; Fiber: 6g; Protein: 3g

Smoky Scalloped Potatoes

You have never tasted scalloped potatoes like these: layers of Yukon gold potatoes, sweet potatoes, smoked Gouda, and sour cream.

Preparation time: 25 minutes
Cooking time: 6 to 8 hours (LOW) or 3 to 4 hours (HIGH)

Ingredients

Nonstick cooking spray
2 cups shredded smoked Gouda cheese or American cheese (about 8-ounces)
1 can (10-3/4-ounce) condensed cream of celery soup
1 carton (8-ounces) sour cream
1/2 cup vegetable broth
1-1/2 pounds Yukon gold potatoes, thinly sliced (about 5 cups)
1-1/2 pounds sweet potatoes, peeled and cut into 1/4 inch slices (about 5 cups)
1 large onion, sliced

Directions

Lightly coat the inside of a 4-1/2 or 5 quart slow cooker with cooking spray.

In a medium bowl, combine the cheese, soup, sour cream, and vegetable broth and set aside.

In the prepared slow cooker, layer half of the potatoes and half of the onion. Top with half of the soup mixture, spreading evenly. Repeat the layers.

Cover and cook on LOW for 6 to 8 hours or on HIGH for 3 to 4 hours.

Makes 10 servings.

Per Serving

Calories: 265; Fat: 12g; Cholesterol: 26mg; Sodium: 612mg; Carbohydrate: 33g; Fiber: 4g; Protein: 8g

Conclusion

I sincerely hope that these recipes will help you discover and appreciate the amazing versatility of the slow cooker! And remember, your imagination is the only limit when it comes to creating delicious slow cooked vegetarian meals. Don't be afraid to adapt your recipes to taste and to try different combination of spices.

If you enjoyed this cookbook, then you may also enjoy my other books:

- Vegetarian Slow Cooker Recipe Book: 30 Easy Set It & Forget It Meals

- Pressure Cooker Recipe Book: Fast Cooking Under Extreme Pressure

- Slow Cooker International Cooking: A Culinary Journey of Set It & Forget It Meals

- 5 Ingredients 15 Minutes Prep Time Slow Cooker Cookbook: Quick & Easy Set It & Forget It Recipes

For more information about myself and to enjoy more amazing recipes, please follow these links:

- Maria Holmes author page at www.amazon.com

- www.holmescookedmeals.com

- Holmes Cooked Meals Facebook page

I will be writing and publishing more cookbooks in the future, so please stay tuned. But for now, I would like to thank you for helping me and supporting my efforts to share my passion for cooking.

Thank you!

Index

Apple-Buttered Sweet Potatoes 123
Apple-Pecan Sweet Potatoes 61
Balsamic Root Vegetables 136
Black Bean Enchilada Casserole 75
Blackberry Dumplings 109
Breakfast Prunes with Orange Marmalade 35
Burgundy Mushrooms 59
Butterscotch Fondue 115
California Vegetable Casserole 128
Candy Bar Fondue 117
Cauliflower and Broccoli in Swiss Cheese Sauce 133
Champagne Poached Pears 97
Cheese Fondue 113
Cheesy Succotash 131
Cinnamon Apples 95
Cowboy Rice and Beans 126
Cranberry and Maple Syrup Oatmeal with Pears 33
Creamy Corn and Roasted Red Peppers 135
Creamy Leek and Potato 42
Creamy White Bean Spread 13
Curried Vegetables 77
Dutch Apple Pudding Cake 99
Easy Cherry Cobbler 111
Easy Vegetable Chili Medley 51
Easy Vegetable Pot Pie 72
Fruit and Whole-Grain Breakfast Cereal 34
Fruit Compote 94
Gingerbread Pudding Cake 88
Green Bean Casserole 65
Hazelnut-Pear Oatmeal 36
Herbed Wild Rice 124
Hoisin-Garlic Mushrooms with Red Sweet Peppers 15
Hot Fudge Sundae Cake 107
Hot Wine to Warm You 20
Hot Zombies 28
Lemon-Pesto New Potatoes 129
Lemony Artichoke Dip with Creamy Swiss Cheese 17
Mexican Fondue 119

Mixed Berry Pudding Cake 92
Mozzarella Marinara Spread 12
Old Fashioned Rice Pudding 101
Orange-Caramel Pudding Cake 90
Pasta with Eggplant Sauce 70
Pizza Fondue 121
Potato and Double Corn Chowder 46
Ratatouille 63
S'More Fondue 116
Saucy Green Beans and Potatoes 132
Sherried Fruit Compote 31
Smoky Scalloped Potatoes 137
South Indian Lentils with Curry Leaves 68
Spiced Cauliflower and Potatoes 73
Spicy Aztec Chili Hot Chocolate 24
Spicy Chipotle-Orange Squash 57
Spicy Vegetable Chili con Queso 10
Spicy Vegetable Chili 54
Squash and Apple Bisque 44
Triple-Chocolate Peanut Butter Pudding Cake 103
Tropical Apricot Crisp 105
Tropical Stuffed Cabbage Rolls 85
Ultimate Macaroni and Cheese 83
Vegetable Minestrone 40
Vegetable Tortellini 38
Vegetarian Chili with Baked Tortilla Strips 52
Vegetarian Gumbo 50
Vegetarian Irish Stew 48
Vegetarian Spaghetti Sauce 79
Warm Mulled Cranberry Punch 26
Warmed Spiced Citrus Cider 22
Western Beans 134
Winter Vegetable Risotto 81

Made in the USA
Monee, IL
16 January 2021